John D Brandt

**Gunnery Catechism, as Applied to the Service of Naval Ordnance**

Adapted to the Latest Official Regulations, and Approved by the....

John D Brandt

**Gunnery Catechism, as Applied to the Service of Naval Ordnance**
*Adapted to the Latest Official Regulations, and Approved by the....*

ISBN/EAN: 9783337157937

Printed in Europe, USA, Canada, Australia, Japan

Cover: Foto ©ninafisch / pixelio.de

More available books at **www.hansebooks.com**

# GUNNERY CATECHISM,

AS APPLIED TO THE

## SERVICE OF NAVAL ORDNANCE.

ADAPTED TO

THE LATEST OFFICIAL REGULATIONS,

AND APPROVED BY THE

BUREAU OF ORDNANCE, NAVY DEPARTMENT.

By J. D. BRANDT,

FORMERLY OF U. S. NAVY.

NEW YORK:
D. VAN NOSTRAND, 192 BROADWAY.

1864.

# CONTENTS.

|  | PAGE |
|---|---|
| Calls for assembling at Quarters, | 5 |
| Broadside Guns, | 9 |
| Manual Exercise, | 13 |
| Exercise of Pivot Guns, | 34 |
| Manning all the Broadside Guns, | 52 |
| General Questions on the Gun Exercise, | 59 |
| Different Kinds of Firing, | 62 |
| Quick Firing with Broadside Guns, | 66 |
| Shifting Trucks, | 68 |
| Shifting Breeches in Action, | 68 |
| The Use of Sights, | 69 |
| The Use of Primers and Fuzes, and of Projectiles from Smooth Bore Guns, | 79 |
| Rifled Cannon and Projectiles, | 95 |
| Service of Magazines, | 101 |
| Passing Powder, | 106 |
| Shell Rooms, | 108 |
| Guns and Carriages, | 109 |
| The XV-inch Guns, | 116 |
| Mortars, and Mortar Practice, | 120 |
| Boat Guns and Exercise, | 133 |
| Gunpowder, | 153 |
| Housing Guns, | 156 |
| Getting in Guns on Covered Decks, | 158 |
| General Questions on Gunnery, | 165 |
| Range Tables, | 176 |
| Tables of Charges, Weights, etc., | 177 |

BUREAU OF ORDNANCE,
NAVY DEPARTMENT.

WASHINGTON CITY, JULY 30th, 1864.

SIR :—

Your "CATECHISM OF GUNNERY, as applied to the service of Naval Ordnance," having been submitted to the examination of ordnance officers, and favorably recommended by them, is approved by this Bureau.

I am, Sir,
Your obedient servant,
H. A. WISE.
*Chief of Bureau.*

MR. J. D. BRANDT,
WASHINGTON, D. C.

# GUNNERY CATECHISM.

### CALLS FOR ASSEMBLING AT QUARTERS.

*Q.—How are all hands called to quarters?*
*A.*—By beat of drum.

*Q.—What is the call for Inspection?*
*A.*—The ordinary Beat.

*Q.—For exercise at General Quarters without powder?*
*A.*—First, *one* roll. Then, the ordinary beat.

*Q.—For actual Battle or Exercise at General Quarters with powder?*
*A.*—The beat quick.

*Q.—When at quarters, what is the signal for Silence and Attention?*
*A.*—A roll of the drum.

*Q.—Must all firing then cease?*
*A.*—Yes, and the next order waited for.

*Q.—How do the men assemble for inspection or general exercise in port?*
*A.*—Unless otherwise ordered, they go first to the starboard guns on spar deck, the port guns on

main deck, and so on to the starboard and port guns on the decks below.

*Q.—How do they assemble at sea?*
A.—They first go to the weather guns.

*Q.—If the ship be dead before the wind?*
A.—They go to the same sides as in *port*.

*Q.— When assembled for Inspection, what should be the exercise?*
A.—To see that guns and everything belonging to them are in order and place.

*Q.—Anything else?*
A.—The men should be mustered at stations as Boarders, Pikemen, Sailtrimmers and Firemen; and practised in shifting from side to side, and in taking places for fighting both sides at once.

*Q.— On assembling for exercise at general quarters without powder, after men are mustered and reports made, what is the order?*
A.—"Cast loose and provide."

*Q.—How is this done?*
A.—The starboard watch cast loose and provide the odd numbered guns, and the *port* watch the even numbered guns. The 1st parts of guns' crews on *starboard side* casting loose and providing the *starboard*, and the 2nd parts the *port* guns. The 1st parts of guns' crews on the *port side* the *port*, and the 2d parts the *starboard* guns.

*Q.—In securing?*

*A.*—The same order is observed.

*Q.— When all the guns are thus cast loose and provided, what next?*

*A.*—The luffs of tackles are choked or hitched, and men return to guns at which they were mustered and await orders.

*Q.— When the Beat for actual battle is made, what do the guns' crews do without waiting for orders?*

*A.*—Provide and cast loose at once, without waiting for further orders, or to be mustered.

*Q.— What is the call for Boarders to go to spar deck?*

*A.*—By the rattle and the verbal order repeated by every officer of division.

*Q.—How do they form?*

*A.*—On the side opposite to that engaged.

*Q.—Do all Boarders go to the spar deck on the first call?*

*A.*—No—only the *first* Division.

*Q.—If the call is repeated before the 1st Division return to their guns?*

*A.*—Then the second division go.

*Q.— What is the call for Pikemen?*

*A.*—Sounding the gong.

*Q.—Where do they go?*

A.—They all go to the spar deck, armed with muskets.

*Q.—How are " all hands " called to repel Boarders?*

A.—By springing the rattles and sounding the gongs together, and by verbal order.

*Q.—How are Sailtrimmers called?*

A.—By passing the word for the particular division wanted.

*Q.—What is the call for Firemen?*

A.—By striking the ship's bell rapidly, and verbal order.

*Q.—What is the " Fire alarm " at all times?*

A.—The rapid ringing of the bell.

*Q.—Where do the crew go then?*

A.—They immediately assemble at quarters and await orders.

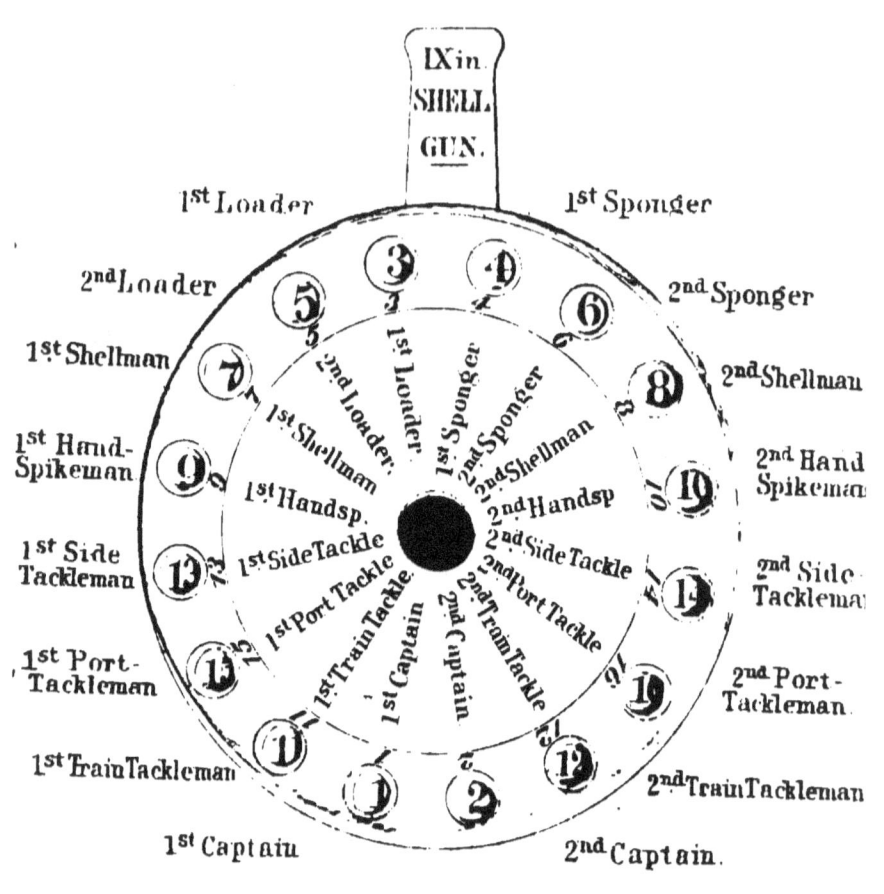

Diagram Showing the manner of shifting Stations in Exercise, in order to drill each of the Guns Crew in all the duties.

# BROADSIDE GUNS.

**Stations and Gun Numbers. IX-in. Shell Gun.**

*Q.—How many men are required to work a IX-in. gun in broadside?*

*A.*—Sixteen men and a Powderman.

*Q.—Repeat the stations and Gun-numbers, commencing with the First Captain.*

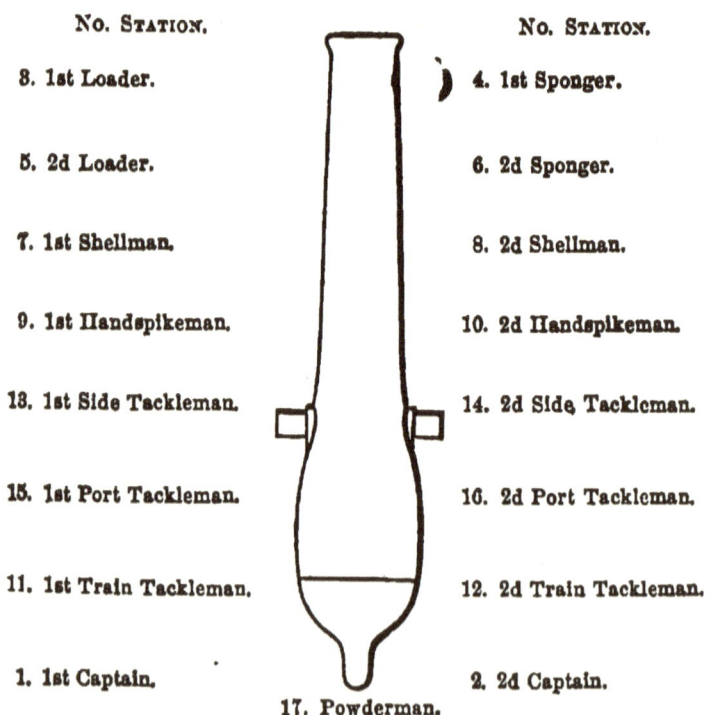

| LEFT SIDE OF GUN. | RIGHT SIDE OF GUN. |
|---|---|
| No. Station. | No. Station. |
| 3. 1st Loader. | 4. 1st Sponger. |
| 5. 2d Loader. | 6. 2d Sponger. |
| 7. 1st Shellman. | 8. 2d Shellman. |
| 9. 1st Handspikeman. | 10. 2d Handspikeman. |
| 13. 1st Side Tackleman. | 14. 2d Side Tackleman. |
| 15. 1st Port Tackleman. | 16. 2d Port Tackleman. |
| 11. 1st Train Tackleman. | 12. 2d Train Tackleman. |
| 1. 1st Captain. | 2. 2d Captain. |

17. Powderman.

*Q.—How do the men stand at the gun before commencing the exercise?*

*A.*—The even numbers on the right side—the odd numbers on the left side—Powderboy in the rear.

*Q.—Name the order in which they stand commencing nearest the ship's side?*

*A.*—Right—No. 4, 6, 8, 10, 14, 16, 12, 2.
Left—No. 3, 5, 7, 9, 13, 15, 11, 1.

*Q.—How do they face?*
*A.*—In-board.

*Q.—Suppose a gun has only 14, or 12 men and a Powderboy, what numbers are omitted?*
*A.*—The higher numbers.

*Q.—Are the stations and duties of the rest changed?*
*A.*—No.

*Q.—With a gun's crew of 10 men, who becomes train-tackleman?*
*A.*—No. 10.

*Q.—Who then handles the handspike?*
*A.*—No. 2.

*Q.—Are the stations and duties of the other numbers changed?*
*A.*—No.

*Q.—With a gun's crew of 8 men, who becomes train-tackleman?*
*A.*—No. 8.

*Q.—Who also attends the handspike?*
*A.*—No. 2.

*Q.—Are the duties of the rest changed?*
*A.*—No.

*Q.—With a gun's crew of six men, are there any changes?*
*A.*—No. 5 also acts as shotman, and No. 2 must attend handspike and train-tackle. The rest remain unchanged.

*Q.—You have given the numbers and stations of the men at the broadside guns. Have they any other stations, and what are they?*
*A.*—Yes. They are stationed also as Boarders, Pikemen, Firemen, Sailtrimmers and Pumpmen.

*Q.—What are the arms used by the men at the guns?*
*A.*—Swords, pistols, pikes, muskets, and battle axes.

*Q.—Commencing with No. 1, name the other stations with the arms of each man, for a gun's crew of 16 men?*
*A.*—No. 1, Second Boarder, sword and pistol.
No. 2, First Boarder, sword and pistol.
No. 3, Second Boarder, sword and pistol.
No. 4, Second Boarder, sword and pistol.
No. 5, First Boarder, sword and pistol.
No. 6, First Boarder, sword and pistol.
No. 7, Second Pumpman, battle-axe.

No. 8, First Pumpman, battle-axe.
No. 9, Second Boarder, sword and pistol.
No. 10, First Boarder, sword and pistol.
No. 11, Fireman, battle-axe.
No. 12, Sailtrimmer, musket and battle-axe.
No. 13, Pikeman, musket and pike.
No. 14, Pikeman, musket and pike.
No. 15, Pikeman, musket and pike.
No. 16, Pikeman, musket and pike.

*Q.— With a gun's crew of 14 men is there any change?*

*A.*—Yes. No. 10 becomes a pikeman, and is armed with a pike and musket, the rest are the same.

*Q.— With a gun's crew of 12 men what changes?*

*A.*—Nos. 7 and 9 become *pikemen*, and are armed with pike and musket, the rest are the same as with a crew of 14 men.

*Q.— With a gun's crew of 10 men?*

*A.*—No. 5 becomes pikeman, (musket and pike.)
No. 7 becomes fireman, (battle-axe.)
No. 10 becomes train-tackleman, (musket and battle-axe.)
The rest are the same as with a crew of 12 men.

*Q.— With a crew of 8 men?*

*A.*—No. 6 becomes pikeman, (musket and pike.)
No. 7 becomes pumpman, (battle-axe.)
No. 8 becomes train-tackleman and fireman, (musket and battle-axe.)

And No. 2 handles handspike.
The rest are the same as with a crew of 10 men.

*Q.— With a crew of 6 men?*

*A.*—No. 4 becomes pikeman, (musket and pike.)
No. 6 becomes fireman, (musket and battle-axe.)
No. 5 becomes shot and pumpman, (battle-axe.)
No. 2 handles handspike and train-tackle.

## MANUAL EXERCISE.

**Broadside Guns on One Side. IX-in. Shell Gun.**

*Q.—How many words of command are there in this exercise?*

*A.*—Ten.

*Q.—Name them?*

*A.*—1. Silence! Man starboard (*or port*) guns!
2. Cast Loose and Provide!
3. Run In!
4. Serve Vent and Sponge!
5. Load!
6. Run Out!
7. Prime!
8. Aim!
9. Ready—Fire!
10. Secure!

*Q.*—At the order *"Silence!"* what is to be observed, and why?

*A.*—The strictest silence, in order that the commands and signals may be distinctly heard and seen.

*Q.*—*How is the gun's crew to stand?*

*A.*—No. 1 faces the port; the men, on the right and left, face the gun with their eyes fixed upon No. 1.

*Q.*—" Cast Loose and Provide!" *What are the duties of No. 1?*

*A.*—No. 1 commands, casts loose and middles breeching, placing selvagee straps and toggles amidships; takes off lock cover and hands it to No. 11, buckles on his waist-belt, puts on thumbstall, and sees that everything is ready and the men equipped.

*Q.*— *When the gun is ready for action what does he do?*

*A.*—Sees that the men take their proper places, and reports to officer of sub-division to which he belongs.

*Q.*— *What are the duties of No. 2?*

*A.*—He assists in casting loose and middling breeching; takes off and places amidships sight covers, selvagee straps and toggles; handles quoin; clears lockstring and coils it loosely around the lock; and buckles on his waist-belt.

*Q.—At Friction Carriages, what does he do besides?*

A.—Removes housing chocks.

*Q.—If the gun has an elevating screw, what does he do?*

A.—Elevates the gun to ease lower half port.

*Q.— What are the duties of No. 3?*

A.—Casts loose port laniards; takes away upper half-port, giving it to men on left side of gun to lay amidships; lets down lower half port; puts hand-swab and chocking quoin near ship's side on left side of gun.

*Q.— What are his duties at lower deck guns?*

A.—Casts off port laniards and muzzle-lashings, removes the port bar, hands it to men on left side of gun to lay amidships, and bears out the port.

*Q.—In what does he assist No. 4?*

A.—In taking out the tompion.

*Q.— What are the duties of No. 5?*

A.—Assists to cast loose; puts wads in place; hooks double-block of side-tackle to side training-bolt on left side of gun.

*Q.— What are his duties at Friction Carriages?*

A.—Sees compressor clear and in working order.

*Q.— What are the duties of No. 4.*

A.—Casts loose port-laniards; takes out tompion

and passes it to No. 6, who hangs it amidships; its chocking quoins on right side of gun near ship's side.

*Q.—In what does he assist No. 3 ?*

*A.*—In taking out half ports and letting down lower ones; and on lower decks, removing port bar, bearing out the port and taking off muzzle-lashings.

*Q.— What are the duties of No. 6 ?*

*A.*—He assists in casting loose; hooks double-block of side-tackle to side-training bolt on right side of gun.

*Q.— What is his duty at Friction Carriages ?*

*A.*—Attends right compressor bar.

*Q.— What are the general duties of Nos. 4 and 6 ?*

*A.*—To take down sponges and rammers; take off sponge cap; lay sponges and rammers together on right side of gun, heads towards the breech.

*Q.— Where are the rammers and sponges placed on covered decks ?*

*A.*—In the brackets overhead.

*Q.— What are the duties of 13 and 14 ?*

*A.*—They assist in casting loose, and on lower decks help Nos. 15 and 16.

*Q.— What are the duties of Nos. 7 and 8 ?*

*A.*—They assist in casting loose and go to hatchway to pass loaded shell, if ordered.

*Q.— What are the duties of Nos.* 11 *and* 12 ?
*A.*—To lead out and hook train-tackle.

*Q.— What are the duties of Nos.* 9 *and* 10 ?
*A.*—They take out the handspikes, place the heels under the breech of the gun, and raise it so as to ease the quoin in order to let down the lower half port.

*Q.—In doing this where do they rest their handspikes?*
*A.*—On the steps of the carriage.

*Q.—How do they stand?*
*A.*—Between the handspikes and the side of the ship.

*Q.— Where do they lay their handspikes after performing this operation?*
*A.*—On the deck, in a line with the gun, butts to the rear and clear of the trucks.

*Q.— What are the duties of No.* 17 ?
*A.*—No. 17 goes to his proper scuttle for a passing box, gets it, goes back and stands a little to the left and in rear of the gun.

*Q.—How does he hold his passing-box?*
*A.*—Under his left arm, the cover closely pressed down with his right hand.

*Q.—In providing broadside guns, what do Nos.* 1 *and* 2 *provide?*

*A.*—Nos. 1 and 2 provide themselves with percussion primers, thumbstalls, and priming wire.

*Q.*—*Nos. 3 and 5?*

*A.*—Nos. 3 and 5 provide a bucket of water and a wet swab.

*Q.*—*Nos. 4 and 6?*

*A.*—Nos. 4 and 6 provide rammers and sponges.

*Q.*—*Nos. 7 and 8?*

*A.*—Nos. 7 and 8 provide selvagee and junk wads, and supply the racks with shot as required.

*Q.*—*Nos. 9 and 10?*

*A.*—See handspikes in place, and help to get up shot.

*Q.*—*Nos. 13 and 14?*

*A.*—Nos. 13 and 14 provide sand and water to sprinkle and sand the decks.

*Q.*—*What does the Fireman provide?*

*A.*—Fire bucket and battle-lantern.

*Q.*—*Where are they hung on gun decks?*

*A.*—The lantern at the ship's side, or in rear of and between the guns; the bucket in rear of the gun.

*Q.*—*Where is the bucket placed on spar decks?*

*A.*—On the deck, or hung up in some convenient place in rear of the gun.

*Q.— When is the lantern to be lit?*

*A.*—Only when ordered by the Captain.

*Q.— What does No. 17 provide?*

*A.*—A passing box, either empty or full as directed.

*Q.—How is the Quarter Gunner equipped, and what does he supply?*

*A.*—With two locks, four lockstrings, eight thumbstalls, two boring bits, two priming wires, a shackle punch, and pins, and some old rags; and he must provide from the supply and reserve boxes belts, primer boxes and other articles, and be ready to furnish spare breechings, ladles, worms, and provide the candles for the battle-lanterns when needed.

*Q.— When should the pistols be loaded?*

*A.*—Whenever there is a probability of going into action.

*Q.— The gun being now cast loose and everything provided, what is the next command?*

*A.*—Run In!"

*Q.—How is this done?*

*A.*—By the train-tackle.

*Q.—Manned by what numbers?*

*A.*—Nos. 7, 8, 9, 10, 11, 12, 13, 14, 15, 16, and if necessary, 5 and 6.

*Q.— Who works the roller handspike?*

*A.*—No. 2.

*Q.— Who overhaul the side tackles?*
*A.*—Nos. 3 and 4.

*Q.— The gun being in, what is done to prevent its running out again?*
*A.*—Choke the luff of the train-tackle.

*Q.— Who does this?*
*A.*—No. 12, assisted by No. 11 if there is much rolling motion.

*Q.—Is anything else done to prevent the gun running out?*
*A.*—Nos. 3 and 4 put truck quoins in front of trucks.

*Q.— What is the duty of No. 6?*
*A.*—With his back square to the gun and facing over left shoulder towards No. 4, he takes up the sponge with its head inboard and stands ready to hand it to No. 4.

*Q.— What is the duty of No. 8?*
*A.*—He does the same thing on his side with the rammer.

*Q.—And the rest of the men?*
*A.*—They go to their stations.

*Q.— What is the next command?*
*A.*—"Serve Vent and Sponge."

*Q.—How is this done?*
*A.*—No. 1 serves and then stops vent, No. 4 re-

ceives sponge from No. 6, right hand over, left under, and assisted by No. 3, sends it home, pressing it to bottom of bore; turns it round two or three times so that the worm at its end may take, draws it out and strikes the handle several taps against the muzzle, then hands it back to No. 6 to lay on the deck, or put it over-head on the hooks.

*Q.—After the sponge is withdrawn what does No. 1 do?*
A.—Serves the vent with his priming wire, and closes it again.

*Q.—What is the duty of No. 8?*
A.—Hands rammer to No. 4 as soon as the sponge is taken from him by No. 6?

*Q.—Suppose No. 1 neglects to serve the vent?*
A.—No. 4 must call his attention to it.

*Q.—What is the duty of No. 3?*
A.—He stands ready with the cartridge he has taken from No. 17.

*Q.—What is the duty of No. 5?*
A.—Opens shell box, takes out the shell and stands ready to hand to No. 3.

*Q.—Who assists him?*
A.—No. 7.

*Q.—Why is the vent stopped while the gun is being sponged?*
A.—To put out any burning fragments of cartridges, and prevent them from being forced into the vent.

*Q.—Do you use a wet or dry sponge?*
*A.*—A wet or moist sponge.

*Q.—Why?*
*A.*—It is found to put out burning fragments in the bore more readily and perfectly than a dry sponge.

*Q.—Why is the staff of the sponge struck several times against the muzzle of the gun?*
*A.*—To shake off burning fragments of cartridges which may adhere to it.

*Q.—If any are drawn out of the gun who puts them out?*
*A.*—No. 3, with a wet swab.

*Q.—What is then done?*
*A.*—No. 1 again commands "Sponge."

*Q.—Why does No. 1 serve vent with his priming wire?*
*A.*—To clear it of pieces of cartridge stuff, which may choke it and prevent the primer from exploding the powder.

*Q.—If he finds it choked and cannot clear it with the priming wire, what does he use?*
*A.*—The boring-bit.

*Q.—If that fails?*
*A.*—He must report to the Officer of the Division who will order the vent punch used.

*Q.—If this also should fail?*

*A.*—Recourse must be had to the vent drill, in charge of the Quarter Gunner.

*Q.— What precautions are necessary in using these implements?*

*A.*—They should be used slowly and with great care, because being of steel they are liable to be broken off and thus spike the gun.

*Q.—After the vent is cleared, what should be done?*

*A.*—Sponge the gun again.

*Q.— What precautions should be taken by Nos. 3, 5, and 4, 6?*

*A.*—To keep their bodies as much within the port as possible.

*Q.—And why?*

*A.*—To prevent being picked off by musketry.

*Q.—The gun being sponged, what is the next command?*

*A.*—"LOAD!"

*Q.—Explain the manner of loading by stating the work to be done by the following numbers:*

*No. 3?*

*A.*—Puts cartridge in muzzle, seam from line of vent, small end in, and pushes it well into the bore.

*Q.— Why is it pushed well into the bore?*

*A.*—To prevent the risk of ignition by the blast of an adjacent gun, as sometimes occurs.

*No.* 4?
*A.*—Stands ready with rammer, enters it into muzzle and pushes the charge steadily to bottom of bore.

*Q.— Who assists him?*
*A.*—No. 3.

*Q.—How does he know when the charge is home?*
*A.*—By the mark on the rammer handle.

*Q.—Is the charge to be rammed home?*
*A.*—No. The charge is *on no account to be struck.*

*Q.— What are the further duties of No.* 3?
*A.*—While No. 4 draws the rammer, No. 3 takes shell from No. 5, lifts and enters it, sabot first, into the muzzle, with its fuze out; he then removes the cap from the fuze, passes it along to No. 1, and pushes the shell into the bore.

*Q.— What next?*
*A.*—No. 4 enters rammer, and assisted by No. 3 pushes the shell in until the mark on rammer handle shows it is home.

*Q.—Is the shell struck by the rammer?*
*A.*—No. It is most strictly forbidden to do so.

*No.* 6?
*A.*—Takes rammer from No. 4 and lays it down.

*Q.— While the above has been going on, what preparations are being made by the rest of the gun's crew?*
*A.*—No. 2 ships roller handspike; Nos. 7, 9, 11,

13, 15,—8, 10, 12, 14, 16, man side-tackles; No. 1 feels if vent is clear, and charge home.

*Q.— What are these preparations for ?*
*A.*—The next command.

*Q.—Is there anything else to be attended to ?*
*A.*—Yes. Nos. 5 and 6 assist at the side-tackles, Nos. 3 and 4 attend the truck quoins and keep the breeching clear of fore trucks; No. 12 prepares to tend train-tackle.

*Q.—In heavy rolling of lee guns, who assists No. 12 ?*
*A.*—No. 11, and if necessary with a round turn round all parts of the fall.

*Q.—Is the cap ever to be removed from the fuse of a shell before it has been entered into the gun ?*
*A.*—Never.

*Q.— With high elevations or when rolling, what precaution is to be taken when loading with shell ?*
*A.*—That it does not slip down the bore before the cap is removed from the fuse.

*Q.— Would the fuse ignite with the cap on ?*
*A.*—No.

*Q.—How do you remove the cap ?*
*A.*—By taking hold of the lug with the fore-finger and thumb, first raising it a little and without twisting it.

*Q.*— *Why is the cap passed to No. 1 after it is removed?*
*A.*—To show that the priming has been exposed.

*Q.*—*Are they thrown away?*
*A.*—No. They are preserved and accounted for at the end of the firing.

*Q.*—*In removing the cap what precaution should be taken?*
*A.*—Not to touch the fuse composition with the fingers, for fear of injuring it by moisture.

*Q.*—*If time will admit should the priming be raised?*
*A.*—Yes. With the fuze picker or the point of a knife, in order to make sure of its lighting.

*Q.*—*Is a wad required over a shell?*
*A.*—No. Unless in heavy rolling when a selvagee wad may be used.

*Q.*—*Is a wad required in loading with shot?*
*A.*—Yes. A selvagee wad is placed over it.

*Q.*— *Would half a selvagee wad be sufficient?*
*A.*—Yes. A half or a third would be sufficient to hold the shot in its place.

*Q.*—*The gun being now loaded, what is the next command?*
*A.*—"Run Out!"

*Q.—If the gun is to windward, what is the duty of No. 2?*

*A.*—Heaves up the carriage fully on the roller handspike.

*Q.—Of Nos. 5 and 6?*

*A.*—They assist at side-tackles.

*Q.—Of No. 12?*

*A.*—Tends train-tackle, if the roll of the ship requires it; if not he overhauls it and assists at side-tackles.

*Q.— What are the duties of the other numbers?*

*A.*—Nos. 3 and 4 remove truck quoins, and keep breeching from fouling the fore-trucks; Nos. 7, 9, 11, 13, 15—and 8, 10, 12, 14, 16 set taut side-tackles.

*Q.—If the gun is to leeward and the ship has much rolling motion, what is the danger?*

*A.*—That the gun will run out with a surge unless prevented.

*Q.— What would be the result?*

*A.*—Starting the charge from its seat, and injuring the carriage and ship's side.

*Q.—Then what precaution must you take?*

*A.*—Nos. 11 and 12 must tend the train-tackle, while 7, 9, 11, 13, 15, and 8, 10, 12, 14, 16 start the gun easily; No. 2 in using the roller handspike must be careful to let down the carriage instantly if it begins to move rapidly; Nos. 3 and 4 remove truck quoins and tend breeching.

*Q.—Is there any other precaution which might be taken?*

*A.*—The roller handspike might not be used at all.

*Q.—When the gun is out, what then?*

*A.*—No. 2 swivels roller handspike for training, or removes it altogether if the ordinary handspikes are sufficient.

*Q.—What next?*

*A.*—Nos. 5, 6 choke luffs of side-tackles, while Nos. 3 and 4 place truck quoins in rear of fore trucks if there is much motion.

*Q.—If the training is to be sharp, where is the proper side-tackle to be hooked?*

*A.*—To the further eye-bolt inside.

*Q.—And the train-tackle?*

*A.*—No. 12 unhooks and hooks it again to the proper eye-bolt in the *deck*.

*Q.—The gun being now run out, what is the next command?*

*A.*—" PRIME!"

*Q.—Explain the operation by stating the duties of the following:*
*No.* 1 *?*

*A.*—No. 1 again makes sure the vent is clear,

inserts a primer, and turns down the hammer upon it.

*Q.—Nos. 9, 10?*

*A.*—Take up handspikes and stand at rear of brackets ready to heave up forward or aft.

*Q.—Nos. 13, 14?*

*A.*—In sharp training they assist Nos. 9 and 10.

*Q.—Nos. 3, 5, 7, 11, 13, 15—4, 6, 8, 12, 14, 16?*

*A.*—They man the side-tackles.

*Q.—How does No. 1 make sure of the vent being clear?*

*A.*—By letting the wire down quickly into the charge.

*Q.— Why is the hammer turned down upon the primer?*

*A.*—To prevent its being blown out by the blast of the next gun.

*Q.— What is the next command?*

*A.*—"Aim!"

*Q.—State the duties of No. 1?*

*A.*—Adjusts or verifies sliding bar of rear sight to distance given by officer of division—falls back so as to be clear of the recoil—stands *directly* in the rear of the gun, lock-laniard in hand, face to the port, and his eye ranging over the sights.

*Q.—At what does he aim?*

A.—The water line of the opposing ship.

*Q.—How does he train the gun?*

A.—By voice or sign.

*Q.—State the duties of No. 6?*

A.—No. 6 throws back the lock-hammer and takes hold of lever of elevating screw.

*Q.—Suppose the roller handspike is not used in training, who performs this duty?*

A.—No. 2.

*Q.—In training what words of command are used?*

A.—"Muzzle to right," or "left."

*Q.—When these are given, what is the action?*

A.—The men at the side-tackles haul on the proper one, and Nos. 9 and 10 heave on the handspike.

*Q.—How is the time given to the other numbers for hauling on the fall, by 3 and 4?*

A.—By keeping their eyes on the handspikemen opposite them.

*Q.—The gun being properly trained, what is the next action immediately before firing?*

A.—No. 2 unships roller handspike; Nos. 9, 10 lay down handspikes; Nos. 3, 4 overhaul side-tackles *to mark*, unless the motion is too great; No. 12 overhauls or holds up train-tackle· Nos. 7, 8 remove quoins from trucks. The men go to their stations.

*Q.—The gun being loaded, primed and aimed, what is the next command?*
*A.*—"READY—FIRE!"

*Q.—State how this is done by No. 1?*
*A.*—When sure of his aim No. 1 draws the laniard promptly and firmly.

*Q.—How must he hold the laniard?*
*A.*—Just taut.

*Q.—Does he move from his place while drawing the laniard?*
*A.*—He is never to attempt to move from his place until the gun is fired.

*Q.—When is the proper time to fire?*
*A.*—When the sights bear upon the object.

*Q.—In case the gun does not fire?*
*A.*—The 2d Captain throws back the hammer, clears the vent, and inserts another primer.

*Q.—At the moment of the gun's discharge, what is the duty of Nos. 11 and 12?*
*A.*—They jerk away the parts of the train-tackle, or hook it if it has been unhooked.

*Q.—Of Nos. 3 and 4?*
*A.*—Place quoins in front of trucks.

*Q.—When the gun is not in to a taut breeching?*

*A.*—No. 2 ships roller handspike, and Nos. 7, 8, 9, 10, 11, 12, 13, 14, 15, 16 run the gun in to a taut breeching; then Nos. 3, 4 place truck quoins, and No. 12 chokes luff of train-tackle.

*Q.—What does No. 1 then do?*

*A.*—Puts back hammer and coils up laniard.

*Q.—No. 6?*

*A.*—Takes up sponge.

*Q.—No. 2?*

*A.*—Levels gun for loading, and lays it fair for running out.

*Q.—If the exercise is to cease, what is the next order?*

*A.*—"Secure!"

*Q.—State the duties of No. 1?*

*A.*—No. 1 sees gun laid square in middle of port; hauls breeching through jaws of cascabel to left side of gun, forming a bight over breech and cylinder, (or 1st reinforce), secures the parts with selvagees and heavers; puts in vent plug; lays hammer of lock in its place; coils lockstring around it; and after the gun is secured and the lower half port hauled up, levels the gun by the handspikes or elevating screw, so as to bring all parts of the tackles and breeching taut.

*Q.—What are the duties of No. 2?*

*A.*—He handles the quoin or elevating screw;

assists No. 1 in hauling through and securing breeching; puts covers over locks and sights.

*Q.— What are the duties of Nos. 9 and* 10?
*A.—*Nos. 9 and 10 handle the handspikes in depressing or elevating the gun.

*Q.— What are the duties of Nos. 3 and* 4?
*A.—*Nos. 3 and 4 haul up and secure lower half-ports, hook the double blocks of side-tackles to the eye-bolts at the side of the ports; put in and secure the upper half ports; and No. 3 swabs the deck to collect any loose powder.

*Q.— What are the duties of the men at the side-tackles?*
*A.—*After they are hooked to the proper eye-bolts, they haul the side-tackles taut, stop the parts together with knittles furnished by the quarter gunner, and expend the falls around the breech of the gun, stopping the bights to the eye-bolts in the side.

*Q.— What are the duties of Nos.* 11 *and* 12?
*A.—*They hook the train-tackle to the side-tackle bolts on each side of port, the double block on the left side, and expend the fall round the breech, stopping the parts in with the side-tackles.

*Q.— What is the duty of No.* 17?
*A.—*He returns the spare powder and the passing boxes to the magazine.

*Q.*— *What is the duty of Nos. 7 and 8?*
*A.*—To return the shells and empty shell boxes to the shell rooms.

*Q.*— *Who returns the arms and implements?*
*A.*—Those who provided them.

*Q.*— *What precaution must be taken with the arms before they are sent below?*
*A.*—To unload them, unless otherwise directed.

## EXERCISE OF PIVOT GUNS.

### XI-in. Shell Gun, or 150 pounder Rifle.

*Q.*—*How many men are required to man an XI-in. pivot gun?*
*A.*—25, including Powderman.

*Q.*— *Give the gun numbers and stations on the left side of gun?*
*A.*—No. 3, First Loader.
No. 5, Second Loader.
No. 7, First Shellman.
No. 9, First Front Leverman.
No. 13, First Compressorman.
No. 11, First Rear Leverman.

No. 17,  
No. 19,  
No. 21,  
No. 23,  
} Tacklemen.

No. 15, First Train Leverman.
No. 1, First Captain.
No. 25, Powderman.

*Q.—On the right side ?*

*A.*—No. 4, First Sponger.
No. 6, Second Sponger.
No. 8, Second Shellman.
No. 10, Second Front Leverman.
No. 14, Second Compressorman.
No. 12, Second Rear Leverman.
No. 18,  
No. 20,  
No. 22,  
No. 24,  
} Tacklemen

No. 16, Second Train Leverman.
No. 2, Second Captain.

*Q.—Suppose you have to reduce from 24 and powderman to 20 ?*

*A.*—Omit the four highest numbers.

*Q.—From 20 and powderman to 16 and powderman ?*

*A.*—Omit the four highest numbers.

*Q.—From 16 men and powderman to 12 men and powderboy ?*

*A.*—Omit four highest numbers, but Nos. 7, 8,

and 9 become pikemen, Nos. 11 and 12 compressor and train-levermen in addition to other duties.

*Q.—From* 12 *men and boy to* 10 *men and boy?*

*A.*—Omit two highest numbers; No. 5 becomes pikeman, No. 7 becomes fireman, Nos. 9 and 10 compressor and train-levermen in addition to other duties.

*Q.—What are the words of command in this exercise?*

*A.*—1. SILENCE! CAST LOOSE AND PROVIDE!
2. RUN IN!
3. "SHIFT PIVOT!" (To right or left.)
4. SERVE VENT AND SPONGE!
5. LOAD!
6. RUN OUT!
7. PRIME!
8. AIM!
9. READY—FIRE!
10. SHIFT TO HOUSING PIVOT AND SECURE!

*Q.—At the first command what are the duties of No.* 1?

*A.*—He commands; sees gun cleared and cast loose, circles cleared and swept, tackles hooked, levers shipped, lock and sights in place, elevating apparatus, pivot bolts and compressors in working order; takes off lock cover and hands to No. 23, who lays it clear of circle, and sees all gear and implements ready for use and the men at stations.

*Q.—What does he provide himself with?*

*A.*—Waist belt and primers, priming wire, boring bit and thumbstall.

*Q.—What are the duties of No. 2?*

*A.*—Takes off sight covers and hands to No. 22 to lay clear of circle; takes away rail-chock and helps to cast loose, and sees that men on his side of gun work promptly.

*Q.—What does he provide himself with?*
*A.*—Waist belt and primers.

*Q.—In casting loose, who clear away bulwarks?*
*A.*—Nos. 15, 16, 17, 18, 23, 24.

*Q.—Who cast adrift lashings of gun?*
*A.*—Nos. 3, 4, 11, 12.

*Q.—Who cast loose in-tackles?*
*A.*—Nos. 15, 16.

*Q.—Out-tackles?*
*A.*—Nos. 13, 14.

*Q.—Training-tackles?*
*A.*—Nos. 19, 20, 21, 22, 23, 24.

*Q.—Who provides implements?*
*A.*—Quarter gunner.

*Q.—Who brings powder?*
*A.*—No. 25.

*Q.—Shells, shell-ladle, etc.?*
*A.*—Nos. 7, 8.

*Q.— Who takes down sponge and rammer?*
*A.*—Nos. 5, 6.

*Q.— Who ships fore carriage levers?*
*A.*—Nos. 9, 10.

*Q.—Rear carriage levers?*
*A.*—Nos. 11, 12.

*Q.—Side levers—ship forward?*
*A.*—Nos. 15, 16.

*Q.— Who takes off sight covers?*
*A.*—No. 2, and hands to No. 22.

*Q.— Who fill buckets of water and bring wet swabs?*
*A.*—Nos. 5, 6.

*Q.— What are the duties of Nos. 21, 22?*
*A.*—Hook outer train-tackles to deck as shifting tackles.

*Q.— Of Nos. 23, 24?*
*A.*—They hook these tackles to the slide.

*Q.— Of Nos. 17, 18?*
*A.*—Hook inner train-tackle to deck.

*Q.— Of Nos. 19, 20?*
*A.*—Hook inner train-tackle to slide.

*Q.— Who attend the compressors?*
*A.*—Nos. 13, 14.

*Q.— Who man the in-tackles?*
*A.*—Nos. 11, 15, 17, 19, 21, 23, 12, 16, 18, 20, 22, 24.

*Q.— Who man carriage levers?*
*A.*—Nos. 9, 10 the fore—Nos. 11, 12 the rear.

*Q.— When the trucks are to be brought into play, how should the levers be shipped?*
*A.*—On their axle squares so as to heave upwards, past the centre, and rest against the wood of the carriage, or slide.

*Q.—If kept in place by hand or a pin are they secure?*
*A.*—No. They may still fly back and do mischief.

*Q.—Suppose the levers are hove down?*
*A.*—They are apt to interfere with the tackles.

*Q.— Why is it necessary to mark the levers with a cold chisel?*
*A.*—In order to have a mark to ship them quickly on the proper square.

*Q.—How many men do the fore carriage levers require to work them?*
*A.*—Two at each, because the weight of the gun has most bearing there.

*Q.—Why are buckets of water brought to the gun?*

*A.*—To moisten the sponge.

*Q.—What is the preparation for the next command?*

*A.*—Stand by to run in.

*Q.—What are now the duties of Nos. 13, 14?*
*A.*—Ease compressors and go to in-tackles.

*Q.—Of Nos. 3, 9—4, 10?*
*A.*—Up fore carriage levers, and Nos. 11, 12 the rear ones.

*Q.—Who tend the out-tackles?*
*A.*—Nos. 5, 6.

Second Command—"RUN IN!"

*Q.—Who haul on the in-tackles?*
*A.*—Nos. 11, 13, 15, 17, 19, 21, 23—12, 14, 16, 18, 20, 22, 24.

*Q.—What are the duties of Nos. 5, 6?*
*A.*—They unhook the out-tackle block from slide, to make room for hooking inner train-tackle.

*Q.—Who heave down carriage levers?*
*A.*—Nos 3, 9, and 4, 10 the fore, 11, 12 the rear.

*Q.—What are the duties of Nos. 13, 14?*
*A.*—To tauten compressors.

*Q.—In pivoting, how far can the carriage be moved by one tackle without fleeting?*

*A.*—Not more than the eighth of a circle.

*Q.—Is it dangerous at sea to leave the slide unconfined?*

*A.*—It is, even for an instant.

*Q.— When then must the second tackle be hooked and hauled taut in pivoting?*

*A.*—When the outer-tackle is ablock.

*Q.—In running in, what precaution is necessary?*

*A.*—To ease the out-tackles gradually so as to check any violent movement.

*Q.— Why so?*

*A.*—Because the trucks are fitted with friction rollers, and the gun moves upon them suddenly and rapidly.

*Q.— What is the preparation for the next order?*
*A.*—Stand by to pivot.

*Q.— Who draws fore pivot bolt?*
*A.*—Nos. 3, 4.

*Q.— Up fore slide levers?*
*A.*—Nos. 15, 16.

*Q.— Who man the outer train-tackle?*
*A.*—Nos. 3 or 4, 11 or 12, 5, 6, 9, 10, 13, 14, (15. 17,) or (16, 18,) (19, 21,) or (20, 22,) 23, 24.

*Q.—Who attend the opposite outer train-tackle?*
*A.*—Nos. 19, 3, or 20, 4.

*Q.—What are the duties of Nos. 17, 18?*
*A.*—Stand by to hook inner train-tackle when outer tackle is ablock.

*Third Command*—" PIVOT, TO RIGHT OR LEFT."

*Q.—In performing this operation, who haul on the outer train-tackle?*
*A.*—Nos. 3 or 4, 11 or 12, 5, 6, 9, 10, 13, 14— (15, 17, or 16, 18,) (19, 21, or 20, 22,) 23, 24.

*Q.—Who ease away the opposite train-tackle?*
*A.*—Nos. 19, 3, or 20, 4.

*Q.—What are the duties of Nos. 17, 18?*
*A.*—Hook inner train-tackle to slide and haul taut.

*Q.—Who unhook outer train-tackles?*
*A.*—Nos. 21, 22, 23, 24.

*Q.—What are the duties of Nos. 3, 4?*
*A.*—To put in fore pivot bolt.

*Q.—Of Nos. 19, 20—17, 18?*
*A.*—To shift inner train-tackle to rear of slide, and to deck.

*Q.—Of Nos. 15, 16?*
*A.*—To heave down fore slide-levers, unship and ship them on the rear slide trucks.

*Q.*—*Of Nos. 5, 6?*
*A.*—Hook *out-tackle* block to slide.

*Q.*—*The gun being pivoted, what next?*
*A.*—The men take stations for next order, which if the gun is loaded will be "Run out," if not loaded, "Sponge."

*Q.*—*When the gun is "Run out," what is the first thing to be done?*
*A.*—Shackle the breeching and remove the rear pivot bolt.

*Q.*—*Why is the rear pivot bolt withdrawn?*
*A.*—To allow the gun to be trained.

*Q.*—*Why cannot the rear pivot bolt be withdrawn before the gun is run out?*
*A.*—Because in order to pivot with ease, the gun has been previously run back against the rear hurter.

*Q.*—*Where is the breeching to be shackled?*
*A.*—Always to the ship's side.

*Q.*—*Who shackles the breeching?*
*A.*—Nos. 3, 13—4, 14.

*Q.*—*Who draws the rear pivot bolt?*
*A.*—No. 2.

*Fourth Command*—"SERVE VENT AND SPONGE."

*Q.*—*How is this performed?*
*A.*—In the same manner as with broadside guns,

and the same preparations are made for loading, except that Nos. 7 and 8 open shell-box, take out shell and place in its *ladle* to pass to Nos. 3 and 5.

*Q.*—*Are the same precautions observed in serving and clearing the vent, and in sponging, as with broadside guns?*

*A.*—Precisely the same.

*Fifth Command*—"LOAD."

*Q.*—*How is this operation performed with pivot guns?*

*A.*—In precisely the same manner as with broadside guns, *in all the details*, except, in handling the shell to the muzzle.

*Q.*—*How does it differ in this?*

*A.*—Owing to the weight of the shell, 135 pounds, it is handled with a ladle constructed for the purpose. Nos. 7 and 8 take hold each of a handle of this, lift up the shell and assisted by No. 5, pass it on to Nos. 3 and 4, who enter it into the muzzle, sabot first and fuze *out*.

*Q.*—*Whilst the gun is being loaded what preparations are made?*

*A.*—Nos. 13, 14 ease compressors, if no motion. If there is, they stand ready to ease at next order. The out-tackles are manned by Nos. 19, 21, 23, 17, 15, 11, 13, and 20, 22, 24, 18, 16, 12, 14; the inner tackles tended by No. 2 and quarter-gunner; *fore* carriage levers are grasped by Nos. 3, 9, and 4, 10; and the *rear* by Nos. 11, 12.

*Sixth Command*—"Run out."

*Q.— What circumstances govern the manner of executing this order?*

*A.*—The gun being to windward or to leeward, and the nature of the rolling motion.

*Q.—If the gun is to leeward and there is much motion?*

*A.*—The tendency is to go out with dangerous violence.

*Q.—Describe the manner of running out to leeward, and the duties?*

*A.*—Nos. 5, 19, 21, 23, 17, 15, 13, and 6, 20, 22, 24, 18; 16, 14, haul cautiously on out-tackles; quarter gunner and No. 2, assisted by Nos. 15, 16, hold well back on in-tackles with a turn caught; Nos. 13, 14 ease compressors; Nos. 3, 9, and 4, 10 heave up fore carriage levers; Nos. 11, 12 keep down rear carriage levers, unless wanted.

*Q.—How is the gun run out* to windward?

*A.*—Compressors eased at once, in-tackles slacked, carriage hove up on the trucks, and gun run out by out-tacklemen, assisted by any of the numbers not engaged in other duties.

*Q.— When the carriage is out?*

*A.*—The carriage levers are let down promptly

and unshipped, compressors set and rear slide lever shipped.

*Q.—Explain more fully the danger in running out an XI-in. gun to leeward?*

*A.*—The gun weighs with the carriage about 20,000 pounds, and moves on friction rollers along a metal plate, down an inclined plane. If permitted to get loose and propelled by the motion of the ship it must disable some of the apparatus, and perhaps the carriage itself.

*Q.—On this occasion what is found to be invaluable in checking the gun?*

*A.*—The *preventer* breeching—it is the best safeguard.

*Q.—How should it be fitted?*

*A.*—So that when well stretched it will not permit the fore trucks to ascend on curve of fore hurter.

*Q.—If they do ascend this curve, what damage is done?*

*A*—The compressors are badly strained.

*Q.—What is the difficulty in running out to windward?*

*A.*—None, except in moving so great a weight up the inclined plane.

*Q.—How is it done?*

*A.*—The carriage is released from all checks, all

the available men man out-tackles, and advantage is taken of the roll to windward.

*Q.—What governs the "setting" of the compressors?*

*A.*—Circumstances must always regulate the degree of compression: *to windward*, set them moderately; *to leeward*, not at all; *off the wind*, according to the roll. At all times the compression should allow the muzzle just to come in for sponging and loading.

*Seventh Command—"*Prime."

*Q.—How is this order executed?*

*A.*—No. 1 again makes sure the vent is clear, letting the wire down quickly into the charge. If all right he inserts a primer.

*Q.— What are the preparations for the next command?*

*A.*—Nos. 15, 16 ship slide levers on axles of rear *slide* trucks, and Nos. 13, 15, 17, 19, 21, 23, 5, and 14, 16, 18, 20, 22, 24, 6, man rear train-tackles.

*Q.— Why does the gun captain again insert his priming wire in order to see the vent clear?*

*A.*—To clear the vent of any pieces of cartridge stuff which may have gotten into it.

*Q.—In using the priming wire, what was the old habit?*

*A.*—To keep it in the vent while the gun was being loaded to feel if the charge was home.

*Q.—What is the objection to this?*

*A.*—The wire is very apt to be bent, and thus effectually spike the gun.

*Q.—Have the percussion primers force enough to penetrate the cartridge if it is not pricked?*

*A.*—Yes. But it is always better to prick the cartridge in order to make sure of its being ignited.

*Eighth Command—*"Aim."

*Q.—How is this order executed?*

*A.*—No. 1 adjusts or verifies sliding bar of rear sight to the range, and steps off the slide directly to the rear, with lock-laniard in hand; No. 2 tends elevating screw; Nos. 15, 16 heave up levers of rear slide trucks and the men at train trackles stand by to train the gun, muzzle to right or left, as ordered.

*Q.—How is the sight bar of the XI-in. gun graduated?*

*A.*—To its own charge only.

*Q.—Suppose reduced charges are used?*

*A.*—They will only be used at short distances when the gun needs no elevation, and the bar will be then down entirely, its head resting on the box.

*Q.—How many degrees of elevation are given by one turn of the elevating screw?*

*A.*—One degree, and the screws may thus be of service when the sight bars are not.

*Q.—How many degrees of elevation do the pivot carriages of the XI-in. gun admit?*
*A.*—Twenty degrees.

*Ninth Command*—"READY, FIRE."

*Q.—How is this performed?*
*A.*—No. 1 holds lock laniard just taut, keeps his eye ranging over the sights—but well down to bottom of notch in head of sliding bar and over point of middle sight, and waits until the roll brings them in line with the object; when sure of his aim *draws* the laniard promptly and firmly.

*Q.—Where does he always aim?*
*A.*—At the WATER LINE.

*Q.—How does he direct the training?*
*A.*—By voice or sign.

*Q.—Suppose the primer misses?*
*A.*—No. 2 removes it, clears the vent, throws back the lock and puts in a fresh primer.

*Q.—If the gun, when fired, does not come in far enough for loading?*
*A.*—Ship carriage levers, heave up and run in by in-tackles to a taut breeching. Throw down levers and set compressors.

*Q.—If the firing is to continue, what is the next order?*
*A.*—SPONGE!

*Q.—If not?*

*A.*—Unshackle breeching, run in back to rear hurter for pivoting. Then pivot to right or left; and when amidships, "*In Pivot Bolt*," "*Run Out*" and secure for sea.

*Tenth Command*—"SHIFT TO HOUSING, PIVOT AND SECURE."

*Q.—State how this order is executed?*

*A.*—No. 1 puts in vent plug, wipes and lays hammer of lock in place, coils lock-string around it, puts on lock-cover and sees the gun properly secured, and the implements and spare articles returned to their places.

*Q.—What are the duties of No. 2?*

*A.*—Levels gun, wipes off and relackers rear pivot bolt and elevating screw; puts on sight aprons; puts in rail chocks, and helps to secure lashings and breechings.

*Q.—Of Nos. 3 and 5?*

*A.*—Put in tompion, on muzzle bag, wipe off and relacker front pivot bolt.

*Q.—Of Nos. 4 and 6?*

*A.*—Return rammer and sponge to place and assist in securing.

*Q.—Of Nos. 11 and 12?*

*A.*—Wipe off and relacker levers and eccentrics, secure levers in place, and assist in securing the gun.

*Q.—Of Nos.* 13 *and* 14 ?

*A.*—Wipe off, relacker and tauten compressors, and assist the carpenters in replacing and securing bulwarks.

*Q.—Of Nos.* 7 *and* 8 ?

*A.*—Return empty boxes, shells, and shell-bearer to their places, and help to secure bulwarks.

*Q.— Who returns the spare powder and passing boxes to magazine ?*

*A.*—No. 25.

*Q.— What are the duties of the tacklemen ?*

*A.*—Tauten and secure "In" and "Out" tackles, make up and secure shifting and training tackles on the slide; ship clevis bolts in deck, pass and tauten gun lashings, and, if required, assist in replacing bulwarks.

*Q.— Who return to their places the spare articles and implements ?*

*A.*—The men who provide them.

*Q.—State briefly the manner of transporting a pivot gun from one end of a vessel to the other ?*

*A.*—Pivot and train the muzzle in the desired direction, ship and secure *transporting* trucks, place the chocking quoins, throw the training trucks out of action, compress the gun near middle of slide, hook some of the tackles for dragging, and others, with capstan bars, for guiding and steadying. Remove pivot bolts and transport.

*Q.—Can guns mounted on pivot carriages be fought upon the rear pivot on the common or shifting centre?*

*A.*—Yes. And fired from any point of the traversing circle, *if the elevation is such as not to endanger the decks.*

## MANNING ALL THE BROADSIDE GUNS.

*Q.—How is this done?*

*A.*—By each gun's crew working together and firing alternately a pair of guns on the same side of the deck.

*Q.—Suppose the after gun on a deck has an odd number?*

*A.*—It and its opposite are to constitute a pair, and the crew distributed between them.

*Q.— When the order is given to man both sides, how do the men distribute themselves?*

*A.*—Guns' crews of *starboard* watch man starboard guns, with their first parts at the *odd*, and second parts at the *even* numbered guns; and gun's crews of *port* watch man *port* guns with their first parts at the *even*, and their second parts at the *odd* numbered guns.

*Q.—What are the permament numbers of the gun's crews?*

A.—Nos. 1, 2, 3, 4, 5, 6.

*Q.—What are the rest?*

A.—Shifting numbers.

*Q.—When the guns are cast loose and provided, how does the exercise go on?*

A.—Nos. 1, 2, 3, 4, 5, 6 remain at their respective guns—the "shifting numbers" change at the order to do so from one gun to the other of the pair. The permanent numbers load the guns ready for running out, while shifting numbers are employed at gun about to be fired.

*Q.—What does the powderboy do?*

A.—Supplies both guns worked by the gun's crew to which he belongs.

*Q.—Who assists at side-tackles?*

A.—Nos. 3, 4, 5 and 6.

*Q.—Suppose the gun's crew consists of 14 men?*

A.—Nos. 8, 14 and 10 work the right, and Nos. 13, 11 and 9 the left side-tackles of their pair of guns; No. 12 tends train-tackle in running out and in, and No. 7 passes shot and shell for his pair of guns.

*Q.—With a gun's crew of 16 men?*

A.—The arrangement is the same, with the addition that No. 16 works at the right, and No. 15 at the left side-tackle.

*Q.— With a gun's crew of 10 men?*
*A.*—Nos. 8 and 10 work the right, and No. 9, assisted by Nos. 1 or 2, the left side-tackles of their pairs of guns; No. 7 supplies shot or shell, and No. 10 tends train-tackles.

*Q.— With a gun's crew of 8 men?*
*A.*—No. 7 supplies shot and shell, and works at left side-tackles; No. 8 tends train-tackles and works at right side-tackles.

*Q.— With a gun's crew of 6 men?*
*A.*—There can be no shifting men, and marines or any other available men must be called upon.

*Q.— What preparations are necessary in fighting all the guns?*
*A.*—Luffs of side and train-tackles of guns run in must be choked or hitched round straps of single blocks, and chocking quoins used when necessary.

PREPARATORY COMMANDS AND DUTIES.

*Q.— What is the first command?*
*A.*—"Silence! Man both sides."

*Q.— What is the second?*
*A.*—"Cast loose and provide."

*Q.—State the duties of No. 1?*
*A.*—No 1 attends to the same duties as prescribed

for both Nos. 1 and 2 when providing and working guns on one side only.

*Q.— What else?*

*A.*—Takes off lock and sight covers, places them, and straps and toggles amidships, middles breeching and handles quoin.

*Q.— Who assists him in doing these?*

*A.*—The train-tackleman.

*Q.— What are the duties of* sponger *and* loader?

*A.*—Assisted by side-tackleman and handspikeman, they do the same as in working one side only.

*Q.— What are the duties of shellman?*

*A.*—Besides his other duties, handles the left handspike in freeing the quoin.

*Q.— Of side-tackleman?*

*A.*—He provides sand and water, sprinkles and sands the deck if directed, and helps sponger.

*Q.— Of the train-tackleman.*

*A.*—Hooks train-tackle.

*Q.— Of the fireman?*

*A.*—Provides fire-buckets and lanterns for both guns of a pair.

*Q.— Of the handspikeman?*

*A.*—Aided by the shellman he does the duty of both handspikemen when working one side only.

*Q.*—*Supposing the guns commanded by* 1st *Captain to be loaded and run out; and those commanded by* 2d *Captain to be run in and loaded, what are the words of command to the* 1st *Captain and crew?*

*A.*—Prime! Aim! Fire!
Shifting men—change!
Serve vent and sponge!
Load!

*Q.*—*What are the words of command to the* 2d *Captain and crew?*

*A.*—Run out and prime!
Aim!
Fire!
Shifting men—change!

*Q.*—*Before directing Captains of guns to continue the exercise, what is best to be done?*

*A.*—To confine the commands to three orders only.

*Q.*—*What are these?*

*A.*—First—1st Captain, sponge and load!
2d Captain, aim and fire!
Second—shifting men—change!
Third—1st Captain, aim and fire!
2d Captain, sponge and load!

QUESTIONS ON THE EXECUTION OF THE COMMANDS.

*Q.*—*How is the order* Prime *executed?*

*A.*—The same as in the exercise for one side only.

*Q.—The order Aim?*

*A.*—The same as for one side, except in tending train-tackle, which with a gun's crew of more than 10 men is done by 2d train-tackleman, by the 2d handspikeman with 10 men, and by 2d shotman with less than 10 men; and the train-tackleman must in all cases attend quoin or screw in place of 2d Captain.

*Q.—The order Fire?*

*A.*—The same as fighting one side only.

*Q.—The order, Shifting men—change?*

*A.*—They go promptly from one gun to the other, taking hold of side and train-tackles, and the handspikeman ships his handspike in the training loop.

*Q.—The order, serve vent and sponge?*

*A.*—The same as for one side only, except that the sponging and loading are done by sponger and loader alone; the Captain passes sponge and rammer to sponger, and handspikeman clears sponge head and worm.

*Q.—Run out and prime?*

*A.*—Same as for one side, except that the left handspike alone is to be used by Captain of gun, and the sponger and loader at the gun are to do the duties of 1st sponger and 1st loader in fighting one side.

*Q.—Load with cartridge?*

*A.*—As in the exercise for one side, the loader

and sponger doing the duty of 1st sponger and 1st loader.

*Q.—Load with shot?*

*A.*—The same as for one side, except shellman passes shot and wad to loader; loader and sponger do duty as 1st spongers and 1st loaders, and sponger returns rammer to deck instead of 2d sponger.

*Q.—Secure?*

*A.*—When this order is given and the guns run out, *shifting* men divide into 1st and 2d parts and go to guns of 1st and 2d Captains; handspikeman helped by shellman frees quoin, lowers breech, raises breech and levels gun; train-tackleman handles screw or quoin; Captain hauls breeching through cascable, helped by train-tackleman, who also puts on lock and sight covers, and hooks train-tackle to side-tackle bolts; side-tackleman on side of loader, and shellman on side of sponger unhook double-blocks from side-training bolts and hand them to sponger and loader.

*Q.—Suppose the guns are to be housed?*

*A.*—It is done as in exercise for one side only—handspikeman being aided by shellman in lowering the breech upon axletree, and train-tackleman taking out bed and quoin; port-tackleman lowers port lid, and brings port bar to sponger and loader.

EXERCISE OF BROADSIDE GUNS ON BOTH SIDES AT ONCE BY MANNING ALTERNATE GUNS WITH FULL CREWS.

*Q.—In this exercise, what is the preparatory order?*

*A.*—Silence! man both sides, every other gun with full crews!

*Q.—How will the men distribute themselves?*

*A.*—Gun's crews of the guns of the *starboard* watch man *odd numbered guns* on *starboard* side, and gun's crews of the *port watch* man *even numbered* guns on the *port side*.

*Q.—How is the exercise to proceed?*

*A.*—The same as for guns on one side only.

## GENERAL QUESTIONS ON THE GUN EXERCISE.

### Changing Stations.

*Q.—Is it important that every man of a gun's crew should know the duties of all the other men?*

*A.*—It is important and necessary.

*Q.—How can this be done?*

*A.*—By making each man fleet his station one

place "with the sun," beginning with No. 2 to do the duty of No. 1.

*Q.—Give an example of what the result will then be?*

*A.*—No. 1 moving one place with the sun becomes No. 9; No. 9, 11; No. 11, 15, and so on all round the gun, the number at the muzzle on left side passing over to the place of the one on the right.

*Q.—Suppose you take first a number from the middle of the crew to do No. one's duty?*

*A.*—Then the other numbers must change places as if the numbers before the one chosen had already been exercised.

*Q.—Suppose the order is simply to "load and fire?"*

*A.*—Each man silently performs his appointed duty, in proper order of time, of sponging, loading, running out, training and pointing.

*Q.—How does No. 1 regulate the elevation and depression?*

*A.*—By raising or lowering his hand, and by holding it horizontally and steady when the gun is "well."

*Q.—How does he regulate the training?*

*A.*—By moving his hand to "right" or "left" as required, and bringing it down to his side when it is "well."

*Q.*—*Before firing what is he to do?*
*A.*—To throw his hand well up as a signal for the men to "drop tackles," and is to give the word "fire" as he pulls the lock string.

*Q.*—*Suppose casualties happen at the gun?*
*A.*—No. 1 orders "close up," and proceeds to equalize the crew on each side.

*Q.*—*If the powderman is disabled, who takes his place?*
*A.*—The next highest number.

*Q.*—*Suppose a broadside gun's crew is so reduced that there are not men enough left to work it, how can it be fired?*
*A.*—While it is partially run in.

*Q.*—*What must be done in this case?*
*A.*—Frap the breeching forward of the carriage, the muzzle being kept outside of port; haul taut and secure side-tackles; place chocking quoins against after part of rear trucks; haul taut and secure train-tackle; place wet swabs against forward part of front trucks, and sprinkle the deck with sand or ashes.

*Q.*—*What charges of powder should be used?*
*A.*—The lowest charges.

*Q.*—*What danger is there in such firing?*
*A.*—There is great danger of accident by fire.

## DIFFERENT KINDS OF FIRING.

*Q.— What is meant by "firing at will?*
*A.*—Firing the guns independently of each other.

*Q.— When should the guns be thus fired?*
*A.*—Whenever the object is visible and should always be used in action unless ordered to the contrary, the smoke from one gun not greatly impeding the firing of another.

*Q.— What is "firing in succession?*
*A.*—Firing one gun after another in regular order.

*Q.—How would you commence?*
*A.*—Forward or aft, according as the wind is blowing.

*Q.— When may this firing be used with advantage?*
*A.*—At the commencement of an action, or whenever a steady continuous fire is desired.

*Q.— What is " quick firing?"*
*A.*—By this is meant rapid firing at will, the tangent sight not being raised.

*Q.— When should this firing be used?*
*A.*—When close along side an enemy.

*Q.— When is the firing direct?*
*A.*—When the gun is laid for the projectile to

strike the object, without grazing between the gun and the object.

*Q.— When is this firing to be preferred ?*

*A.*—When the object is so near that the chances of hitting are very great; and also when the intervening surface between gun and object is so rough or irregular that a projectile striking it will lose much of its velocity, and have its direction changed.

*Q.— What does the practice of direct firing require ?*

*A.*—A correct knowledge of distance, with precision of elevation and lateral direction.

*Q.— What is called ricochet firing ?*

*A.*—When the gun is so laid that the projectile makes numerous grazes between gun and object.

*Q.— When can this firing be used with advantage ?*

*A.*—Upon a smooth surface within certain distances.

*Q.—Is the flight of the shot retarded while ricochetting on smooth water ?*

*A.*—No. It is but very little retarded and sweeps close to the surface.

*Q.— What then does ricochet firing require ?*

*A.*—At low elevations only correct lateral direction.

*Q.—Place a sereen, 20 feet high, on smooth wa-*

ter at 1,300 *yards from an XI-in. gun, ricochet a shell with the bore of gun level, how high up will it strike in grazing ?*

*A.*—Not higher than 10 feet

*Q.*—*Suppose the water is rough, how does it affect the ricochet ?*

*A.*—It causes the projectile to deviate, and to bound high.

*Q.*—*Does it affect range and penetration ?*

*A.*—Yes. It makes a very perceptible difference in both.

*Q.*—*At sea, when the surface is not smooth, what are the most favorable circumstances for ricochet firing ?*

*A.*—When the flight of the shot is with the roll of the sea, and the sea is long and regular.

*Q.*—*How far is ricochet firing effective against small objects ?*

*A.*—Up to 2,000 yards.

*Q.*— *When should it commence ?*

*A.*—At not less than 600 yards; at less distances it is preferable to fire direct.

*Q.*—*How far has a shot fired horizontally from a 32-pounder of 33 cwt. on smooth water, with a charge of* $4\frac{1}{2}$ *pounds, ricochetted and rolled ?*

*A.*—About 3,000 yards.

*Q.—With the same gun and charge, and an elevation of 5 degrees, what is the greatest range?*

*A.*—1,800 yards.

*Q.—Do shot ricochet at all with elevations above 5 degrees?*

*A.*—Very rarely, and the bounds are always higher as the elevation is increased.

*Q.—To what description of guns do the foregoing questions and answers apply?*

*A.*—Exclusively to smooth bore guns firing spherical projectiles.

*Q.—Do not the elongated projectiles from **rifled** guns also ricochet?*

*A.*—They do; but they lose all certainty of direction on the re-bound, and their range and penetration is nearly neutralized.

*Q.— What is concentration of fire?*

*A.*—The simultaneous discharge of a number of guns upon some particular part of an object whose distance is known.

*Q.— What is necessary in such cases?*

*A.*—That all the guns which are to fire in this manner should be regulated by one gun, and fired altogether.

*Q.—Is this difficult to accomplish?*

*A.*—Yes. And even if successful would be objectionable on account of the heavy shock.

*Q.—Upon what does the success of this and all other kinds of firing at sea depend?*

*A.*—Upon the skill, judgment and coolness of the captains of the guns.

## QUICK FIRING WITH BROADSIDE GUNS.

*Q.—Can a gun be loaded too rapidly?*

*A.*—Not unless it endangers the crew, or the gun itself.

*Q.—If two hostile ships meet equally manned and equipped, and are so near that exact aim is not necessary, which will have the advantage?*

*A.*—The one that loads the quickest.

*Q.—How should the crews be exercised in order to secure rapidity of loading?*

*A.*—By setting the cartridge, shot and wad home together with one motion.

*Q.—Can this be done with all guns?*

*A.*—Yes. Both chambered and unchambered, except the VIII-in. of 63 cwt. of a pattern earlier than 1851.

*Q.—Is it recommended to load in this manner the IX-in. and higher calibres?*

*A.*—No.

*Q.— Why?*

*A.*—Because nothing would be gained in point of time.

*Q.—How would you prevent the shot in loading thus from rolling on the tie of the cartridge and jamming it?*

*A.*—Shortening the tie as much as possible.

*Q.—How is the loader to know when the charge is home?*

*A.*—By the mark on the rammer handle, which should be plain enough to be known by day or night.

*Q.— What is the word of command?*

*A.*—Load in one motion!

*Q.—Explain the operation?*

*A.*—Loader receives cartridge and puts it in gun, then shell, or shot and wad; sponger and loader shove the whole charge down with the rammer as in ordinary loading. When *home,* the men run gun out quickly, captain clears vent, primes while running out, points and fires as rapidly as he can aim, taking care that the muzzle of the gun is clear of port-sill.

*Q.—If on lower decks?*

*A.*—He must see that the port is triced up clear of the explosion.

## SHIFTING TRUCKS.

*Q.— When can this be required?*
*A.*—Only when the gún is *run in* after firing.

*Q.—How is it done with the Marsilly carriage?*
*A.*—Heave up with roller handspike under end of bracket; handspikemen pass inside of breeching, place handspikes under fore axletree, near truck, and assisted by Nos. 5 and 6, lift the gun; shellman takes off old truck, side-tackleman puts on new.

*Q.— With the ordinary carriage?*
*A.*—To shift a *rear* truck, handspikemen lift under rear axletree; *fore truck*, the opposite *rear* truck should be taken off first, then handspikemen lift under fore axletree.

---

## SHIFTING BREECHINGS IN ACTION.

*Q.— What is the command?*
*A.*—"Sponge! load! shift breechings."

*Q.—Suppose the gun's crew reduced to six men and powderboy, what are the duties?*
*A.*—No 1 hauls taut train-tackle and chokes luff; Nos. 3 and 4 put chocking quoins forward of front

trucks, sponge and load the gun; Nos. 6 and 5 haul taut side-tackles and choke luffs, or if rolling deep, hitch the falls round the straps of blocks, and then unshackle old breeching and shackle new one.

*Q.—Who brings new breeching to the gun?*
*A.*—No. 2.

*Q.—What are the other duties of Nos. 1 and 2?*
*A.*—No. 1 removes old breeching from, and secures bight of new breeching in jaws of cascabel, after gun is sponged; No. 2 passes old breeching amidships, and men resume their duties.

*Q.—When there are more than 6 men at the gun?*
*A.*—Nos. 5 and 6 assist to load, and the additional men help to shackle and unshackle breeching, one doing the work just named for No. 1, so that he may attend to his regular duties.

## THE USE OF SIGHTS.

*Q.—How is the operation of pointing guns facilitated?*
*A.*—By sights prepared and fitted carefully to each gun.

*Q.—Name those ordinarily fitted to guns in the U. S. Navy?*
*A.*—The "reinforce sight," and the "breech sight."

*Q.—Describe the "reinforce sight?"*

A.—It is a fixed piece, of metal, firmly secured on the sight mass between the trunnions.

*Q.—Describe the "breech sight?"*

A.—This is a bar or stem, also of bronze, with a "head," in the top of which is a sight notch.

*Q.—How is it adjusted to the gun?*

A.—It is made to slide in a vertical plane in the sight box fixed to the breech, and is held at any elevation by a thumbscrew.

*Q.—How is it marked?*

A.—It has lines across its face denoting degrees of elevation for all the guns of the old system, each of which is marked with the number of yards at which the projectile fired with a given charge, will strike the point aimed at when that line is brought to a level with top of sight box.

*Q.—With the guns of the new system, how are they marked?*

A.—The lines are marked for the ranges in *even* hundreds of yards.

*Q.—What is the uppermost line on the stem?*

A.—It is marked "level," and is the zero of the other graduations.

*Q.—When this mark is adjusted to the top of the sight box, what does the bottom of the notch in the breech sight and the top of the reinforce sight show?*

A.—The "dispart" of the gun.

*Q.— What is the " dispart ?"*

4.—Half the difference between the diameter at base ring and swell of muzzle, or at any intermediate point on the line of metal.

*Q.—Suppose the gun has a lock piece ?*

*A.*—Then its height above the base ring must be added.

*Q.— When the line of sight coincides with the bottom of notch in the breech sight and the top of the reinforce sight, is it parallel to the bore ?*

*A.*—Yes. And if continued to a distant horizon, the gun is laid level or horizontal.

*Q.—Is the level line on the stem (or bar) made to correspond with the bottom of the " head " when it rests on the sight box, and why ?*

*A.*—Yes. In order to secure a dispart sight in case of accident to the screw in the sight box.

*Q.—Suppose these established sights are not furnished, or have become unserviceable, what must be done ?*

*A.*—Lash a *wooden* dispart sight on the reinforce with a groove in it.

*Q.—In securing this wooden dispart sight, what is particularly to be attended to ?*

*A.*—To get the groove in the same plane with the line of sight marked on the gun.

*Q.— What is the "line of metal?"*

*A.*—A line drawn from top of muzzle to top of base ring.

*Q.—Is the inclination of this line to the axis of bore the same in all guns?*

*A.*—No. It varies even in guns of the same class.

*Q.—In aiming by this "line of metal," how are you apt to be misled?*

*A.*—By giving too much elevation to the piece.

*Q.—How is the vertical plane passing through axis of bore marked upon new guns?*

*A.*—By notches in base ring or over the vent—front sight mass and swell of muzzle.

*Q.—In what relation is this line to the trunnions?*

*A.*—It is at right angles to their axis.

*Q.— When the sliding bar of the breech sight is down with its head resting upon the box, and the bore of the gun is level, what term is used to designate the range?*

*A.*—"Point blank," or "point blank range."

*Q.— What is the true definition of this term?*

*A.*—That point at which a shot fired with its full service charge from a level gun, crosses in its flight the horizontal plane upon which the trucks of the gun stand.

*Q.— What, therefore, does the "point blank" range depend on?*

*A.*—The class of gun, the charge and initial

velocity of the powder, the weight and description of projectile used, and the height of the carriage.

*Q.—What seems to be a more preferable definition of this distance?*

*A.*—"Range at level."

*Q.—Is the definition of the term "point blank" the same in other services?*

*A.*—No. The English define it as the distance from the gun when laid horizontal, eight feet above the plane, to the first graze of the shot; and the French point blank is that point where a shot in its flight intersects a second time the line of metal prolonged. But this cannot apply to our Navy guns, as they have a cylinder from base ring to reinforce.

*Q.—How is the aim always supposed to be directed?*

*A.*—At the water line.

*Q.—Suppose then the object was at point blank range, and, with the sight at "level," you aimed at its water line, where would the shot strike?*

*A.*—Short of the point aimed at by about one-quarter the distance.

*Q.—Suppose, however, you were to aim in this case at the upper part of the enemy's hull?*

*A.*—The shot would then strike a distance below the point aimed at equal to the height of the gun above the water.

*Q.—How then is this source of error avoided?*

*A.*—By marking the sights from 100 yards to the greatest range, and throwing out all consideration of point blank, and all sights are now being so marked.

*Q.—Are sights transferable from one gun to another?*

*A.*—No. Being adjusted and marked to particular guns they should not be transferred to any other, even of the same class.

*Q.—How do you use the sights?*

*A.*—Raise or lower the breech sight to the distance, in yards, of the object aimed at, and set the thumbscrew. Then if the ship is steady, elevate or depress the gun until the line of sight from the BOTTOM of notch in breech sight, the top of front sight and the point to be struck coincide.

*Q.—Suppose the ship has a rolling motion?*

*A.*—The gun must be so laid, after the sight is set for distance, that this coincidence may be obtained at the most favorable part of every roll

*Q.—Why is it very necessary that in ranging the eye over the sights, it should be kept well down to the bottom of the notch in head of sliding bar and over the top of front sight?*

*A.*—To avoid firing too high.

*Q.— When the vessels are moving how should the gun be trained?*

*A.*—It is best to train a little ahead, watching when the object draws in line; then, as the roll brings the piece right in elevation, it is fired.

*Q.—In case the ordinary sights are lost or rendered useless, what kind of firing may be resorted to against ships?*

*A.—Tangent firing.* The distance being known, or estimated, point the gun, with the dispart sight, at that part of the enemy's ship given in the tables corresponding with that distance and class of gun.

*Q.— What other sights are sometimes provided for pivot guns?*

*A.*—Trunnion sights, to be used *only* when the ordinary sights will not give the required elevation.

*Q.—Are they to be depended on?*

*A.*—Only approximately; and all the new guns are now being fitted with side sights similar to the plan adopted for the Parrott system of rifled guns, that is, a breech sight on left side of breech; and a front sight on the left rimbase.

*Q.—Does this permit the guns to be accurately aimed?*

*A.*—Yes. At all elevations.

*Q.— What is the best instrument for approximating distances?*

*A.*—The breech sight-bar.

*Q.—How so?*

*A.*—Because if the shot falls short or exceeds the object, by adjusting the bar and making an allowance of about fifty yards for all causes of variation, the correct distance is soon ascertained by the shot striking the object.

*Q.—Suppose an enemy within point blank range, but his hull cannot be seen, how would you aim and fire?*

*A.*—The guns being laid level I would aim and fire by the flashes of the enemy's guns.

*Q.—How are most naval guns now fitted for elevating them?*

*A.*—With elevating screws.

*Q.—Are beds and quoins still in use?*

*A.*—Yes. But only for guns of the old system.

*Q.—With the bed and quoin, when is the gun level in its carriage?*

*A.*—When the inner, or thick end of quoin is fair with the end of the bed in its place.

*Q.—How is the quoin marked?*

*A.*—On its *side* for degrees of elevation, and on its flat part for depression.

*Q.—In depressing how is the quoin turned?*

*A.*—On its side or edge.

*Q.— When has the gun its greatest safe elevation in the ordinary broadside ports?*

*A.*—When the quoin is removed, and the breech rests on the bed.

*Q.— When has it the greatest depression?*

*A.*—When the quoin is pushed home on its side.

*Q.—How is the quoin prevented from flying out when the gun is fired?*

*A.*—Its *stop* must be properly lodged in the holes in the bed.

*Q.—In using elevating screws, should a quoin be at hand, and why?*

*A.*—Yes. To place under the breech when firing at extreme elevation, in order to relieve the screw of the shock, and prevent a change of elevation; also to take the place of the screw if it is disabled.

*Q.—How is the screw prevented from turning and altering the elevation?*

*A.*—By stopping the lever with a laniard.

*Q.—How is additional elevation or depression obtained, beyond that the port admits of?*

*A.*—By placing inclined planes for the rear and front trucks to recoil upon respectively.

*Q.—The sights being adjusted properly, when is the best time to fire at sea?*

*A.*—If the ship is steady, when the line of sight is brought upon the object, if rolling, a little before.

*Q.—Is it best to fire when the ship is rolling towards the enemy ?*

*A.*—Yes. But if practicable, when the ship is on top of a wave, and just *begins to roll towards* the enemy.

*Q.—If from any cause, after the gun is pointed, the firing is delayed ?*

*A.*—The gun should be pointed again before firing.

*Q.— What is the great object in firing ?*

*A.*—It is to fire *low enough* to strike the hull, and near the *water line.*

*Q.—In general, how should the guns be pointed ?*

*A.*—To strike somewhere between the fore and mizzen masts of an enemy.

*Q.— When quite near ?*

*A.*—Guns of forward division at hull near foremast, and one or two after guns at rudder, if it should be fairly exposed.

# THE USE OF PRIMERS AND FUZES; AND OF PROJECTILES FROM SMOOTH BORE GUNS.

### Primers.

*Q.—How many kinds of primers are there?*
*A.*—Two, percussion and friction.

*Q.—Describe the percussion primer?*
*A.*—It is composed of a quill-tube, capped by a percussion wafer. The tube is filled with fine grained powder, and the wafer is composed of cartridge paper enclosing a layer of fulminate of mercury mixed with a small quantity of mealed powder.

*Q.—How is the wafer preserved from dampness?*
*A.*—By a coating of uncolored shellac.

*Q.—How are the quills inspected?*
*A.*—By first passing them through a gauge rather smaller than the vent of guns.

*Q.—How are they put up for service?*
*A.*—In tin boxes intended to fit the leather primer boxes worn by captains of guns. In action a full box of primers should be delivered to each of them.

*Q.—What is the allowance of primers?*
*A.*—120 to every 100 rounds.

*Q.—What is essential in putting the percussion primer in the vent?*

*A.*—That its head should be placed flat and pressed close upon the vent, in order that the hammer may strike it fairly.

*Q.—Do these percussion primers ever fail to ignite the charge even when fairly struck?*

*A.*—Yes. The lower end of the quill being sealed it occasionally obstructs the jet of flame, which is then dispersed laterally and fails to ignite the charge.

*Q.—What is a good precaution to prevent this?*

*A.*—To pinch the end of the tube before putting it in the vent.

*Q.—If a primer should be found too large for the vent?*

*A.*—Throw it away, never attempt to force it down.

*Q.—If the lockstring is not properly pulled, and the head of the primer is only crushed without exploding it?*

*A.*—A second and stronger pull may explode it.

*Q.—If, however, this should fail?*

*A.*—Draw the tube of the primer out, if possible, before using the priming wire to clear it.

*Q.—In case either lock or primer should fail, what recourse have you?*

*A.*—To the "friction primers," or to the "spur tubes."

*Q.—Describe a friction primer?*

*A.*—It consists of a tube charged with powder, having a spur fastened to its top containing friction powder.

*Q.—How is it exploded?*

*A.*—By means of a slider of wire which is pulled out of the spur by a laniard.

*Q.—How are they packed?*

*A.*—In tin boxes, the same as percussion primers.

*Q.—Describe the manner of using the friction primers in firing a gun?*

*A.*—No. 1 raises the wire loop up in a line with the spur, places the tube in the gun, spur towards muzzle, hooks the laniard into the wire-loop, and pulls it when ready to fire the gun.

*Q.—Does it require as strong a pull as with the lock and* percussion *primer?*

*A.*—Not quite so strong a pull.

*Q.— What insures the downward passage of the fire in* friction *primers?*

*A.*—The hole bored through the middle of the powder in the tube.

*Q.—Is there any objection to the use of these friction primers on board ship?*

*A.*—Yes. They are apt to fly and injure the men standing near, particularly on covered decks.

*Q.— What is the imperative rule in relation to the stowage of percussion and friction primers?*

*A.*—They are on no account to be placed in the magazine.

*Q.— What is a "spur tube?"*

*A.*—A quill filled with mealed powder, and having a quill spur also filled with powder.

*Q.—How is it exploded?*

*A.*—It is inserted into the vent, spur forwards, No. 2 exposes the priming which is fired by the match.

*Q.— What insures its igniting the charge?*

*A.*—Like the friction primer, the powder in the tube is bored out in the middle.

*Q.— What precaution is necessary in using the match to fire the quill tube?*

*A.*—To touch the priming forward of the vent; otherwise the blast from it would blow away the match.

### Fuzes.

*Q— What kind of fuzes are used with spherical shells in the Navy?*

*A.*—They are generally fitted with what is known as the "Navy Time Fuze."

*Q.— What are the exceptions?*

*A.*—The 24 and 12-pounder howitzer shells, and all shrapnel.

*Q.— What is the "Navy Time Fuze?"*

*A.*—It is composed of a composition driven in a paper case, and then inserted in a metal stock which is screwed into a bouching fitted to the shell.

*Q.— What protects the flame of the burning fuze from being put out on ricochet?*

*A.*—A *water cap* of peculiar construction.

*Q.— What protects the priming and fuze from moisture and accidental ignition?*

*A.*—A "safety cap," or patch of lead.

*Q.—Is there any other appendage to the fuze?*

*A.*—Yes. A "safety plug" at the lower extremity.

*Q.— What is the use of this "safety plug?"*

*A.*—In the event of the accidental ignition of the fuze after it is uncapped it prevents the communication of fire to the powder in the shell.

*Q.— Then how is it detached?*

*A.*—By the shock of the gun's discharge.

*Q.— What are the times of burning of the Navy time fuze?*

*A.*—$3\frac{1}{2}$, 5, 7, 10, 15 and 20 seconds.

*Q.—Are any fuzes of greater length supplied?*

*A.*—Yes. Fuzes driven in paper cases.

*Q.— What is the general working fuze?*

*A.*—The 5 second fuze; and for greater or less distances this may be drawn and another substituted.

*Q.— Will ricochet on water put out the Navy time fuze?*

*A.*—Very rarely, and towards the end of its flight, when fired direct, it frequently acts by concussion.

*Q.— What should govern the use of fuzes?*

*A.*—The time of burning should suit the distance of the object; the shorter times being of quicker composition are more certain.

*Q.—Can these fuzes be shortened, and how?*

*A.*—Unscrew the water cap, back out the paper case, cut off from the *lower* end with a fine saw or sharp knife the proportional part required, and insert the upper part in the stock again; then screw on the water cap, or it may be bored out from the lower end with a small hand drill to the proper depth.

*Q.— What kind of fuzes are used in shrapnel, and the 24-pounder and 12-pounder howitzer shells?*

*A.*—The Bormann fuze.

*Q.—Describe it?*

*A.*—The Bormann fuze is a thick circular disc made of an alloy of tin and lead. It has a screw thread cut upon its edge to secure it to the fuze hole of the projectile. The composition is driven into a circular groove on the under side, and covered with a plate of tin. The upper side is divided into seconds and quarter seconds.

*Q.*—*How is the fire communicated from this fuze to the powder in the shell?*

*A.*—Besides the composition it has a priming magazine which explodes and drives its flame into the shell.

*Q.*—*How is this fuze lit?*

*A.*—It is cut, or opened with the fuze cutter at the required number of seconds, thus exposing the composition to the flame of the charge in the gun.

*Q.*—*What precaution is necessary?*

*A.*—Always to cut to the *right* of the mark on the index plate.

*Q.*—*Suppose the cut is made into the magazine itself?*

*A.*—The shell would be exploded at the muzzle.

*Q.*—*Cannot this property of the fuze be made useful?*

*A.*—Yes. In case of a deficiency of canister, if the fuze of the shrapnel is so cut it acts as a very efficient substitute.

*Q.*—*How should the shell fitted with the Bormann fuze be placed in the gun?*

*A.*—Always with the cut of the fuze up.

*Q.—Why so?*

A.—Because in this position it is more certain of being touched by the flame of the charge as it rushes over the top of the shell.

*Q.—What kind of fuzes are used at present with rifled projectiles?*

A.—The percussion and time fuzes of Hotchkiss, Shenckl, Parrott and Tice.

*Q.—Are time fuzes unreliable in rifle guns?*

A.—Generally so, especially with expanding projectiles.

*Q.—And why?*

A.—Because they cut off the flame from the fuze.

*Q.—Where is the best effect of a percussion fuze obtained?*

A.—In firing into a mass of timber.

*Q.—What is essential to the proper action of percussion fuzes?*

A.—That the shells should strike against a substance sufficiently hard, and always point foremost.

*Q.—If it is desired to explode a shell in front of, or in the midst of a body of troops, what kind of fuze is to be used?*

A.—The time fuzes, with both shell and shrapnell.

*Q.—Do time fuzes burn with greater rapidity in shell thrown from rifled cannon?*

A.—They do, because being in front they are subjected to greater pressure from the air,

*Q.—Rifled shell then require a time fuze especially adapted to them?*

*A.*—Yes. Unless the Navy time fuze is used, which being always burnt under a pressure greater than that caused by the motion of the shell, burns with the same rapidity in all classes of projectiles.

*Q.—To what is this equal rate of burning due?*

*A.*—To the water caps, which obstructs the issue of the flame. The paper case Navy fuzes must therefore always be put in the Navy fuze stock and the water cap be screwed in over it.

*Q.—Before the invention of the present time fuze, how were they prepared?*

*A.*—The composition was driven into a wooden stock by drift and mallet, and this stock was then driven into the fuze hole, and the shell loaded through a smaller hole made in it for the purpose.

*Q.—How far will the 5 second Navy time fuze carry a shell?*

*A.*—Up to about 1,400 yards. Beyond that the 10 and 15 second fuzes are to be substituted.

*Q.—How are the different kind of fuzes made up?*

*A.*—In separate packages, distinctly marked with the kind and length of the fuze.

**Projectiles for Smooth Bore Cannon.**

*Q.—Name the different kinds of projectiles fired from smooth bore guns in the Navy?*

*A.*—Solid spherical shot, shells, shrapnel, grape, and canister.

*Q.—If in loading a shot should stick in the bore?*
*A.*—No attempt is made to ram it down, but it should be drawn by the ladle or otherwise.

*Q.—In service are shot saboted?*
*A.*—No.

*Q.—Are guns ever loaded with more than a single shot at a time?*
*A.*—Never, unless expressly ordered by the captain.

*Q.—Are solid shot fired from shell guns?*
*A.*—They may be for a limited number of fires, and only when ordered by the captain.

*Q.— When should double shotting be resorted to?*
*A.*—Only against an enemy directly abeam.

*Q.—At what distance is double shotting with 32-pounders of 46 cwt. and upwards effective against a ship?*
*A.*—At not more than 300 yards; beyond that their divergence is too great.

*Q.— With 32-pounders of less than 46 cwt.?*
*A.*—At not more than 200 yards.

*Q.— What is a spherical shell?*
*A.*—A hollow globe of iron, filled with powder, and fitted with a fuze.

*Q.—How are they fitted for service?*
*A.*—They are strapped to a disc of wood, called

a sabot, by strips of tin, then painted and put up in suitable boxes.

*Q.— What is done to ensure their fitting the bore properly?*

*A.*—They are accurately gauged before reception from the foundries.

*Q.— What is the use of the sabot?*

*A.*—To keep the fuze in its place *outwards* in the axis of the bore.

*Q.—For what reason?*

*A.*—Because, if otherwise, the fuze might turn towards the cartridge, be driven in, and explode the shell in the gun.

*Q.—Is a gun ever loaded with two shells?*

*A.*—No. The firing of two loaded shells should *never* be practised.

*Q.— What kind of powder is used in filling shells?*

*A.*—Musket powder of the highest initial velocity.

*Q.—Is it necessary to fill the shell?*

*A.*—Yes. The shells should be *filled*, and the powder well shaken down, leaving only room for the fuze.

*Q.— What care is necessary with shells on board ships, especially steamers?*

*A.*—That their condition, and especially that of the fuzes should be frequently examined into, taking out a fuze occasionally in order to see if it has been injured by the moisture, and to have all damaged fuzes replaced by fresh ones from the stock of spare ones on board.

*Q.—In changing the fuzes what care is necessary?*

*A.*—To strike the side of the shell gently to detach the powder from the fuze, to work very slowly in unscrewing, and not to try to overcome any unusual resistance.

*Q.—What precautions are necessary, and how are shells loaded and fuzed on board ship?*

*A.*—A properly secured place is first prepared, and the shells with the powder and fuzes brought there. The shells are then examined to see that they are clean and thoroughly dry, inside and out. Take great care to remove every particle of dirt, sand, or fragment of iron from the inside. Then pour through a funnel the prescribed charge of powder into the shell. If any grains remain sticking to the threads of the bouching, brush them off; put a light coat of lacker for small arms, or sperm oil on the thread of the bouching and fuze stock, and screw the latter carefully in with the fuze wrench. Shell should never be loaded, or their fuzes shifted, in the shell room.

*Q.—How are shells emptied?*

*A.*—Place them on a bench with a hole in it to receive and support the inverted shell, and have a wooden vessel underneath to receive the powder.

*Q.—Suppose the powder in the shell has become caked?*

*A.*—Drown and remove it by washing out the shell.

*Q.—How are loaded shell known?*

*A.*—They are painted *red*, and put in boxes marked with a red cross, and the lengths of the fuzes painted on the boxes in black.

*Q.—What other precautions are to be always taken with loaded shells?*

*A.*—They are to be always handled with great care whether in or out of the boxes, especially any that are fitted with percussion fuzes.

*Q.—When returned from ships are percussion shells allowed to go at once into the shell-houses?*

*A.*—Not until their fuzes have been removed and the fuze hole plugged.

*Q.—Where are shells for boat guns stowed on board ship?*

*A.*—In the shell-rooms in their appropriate boxes.

*Q.—What fuzes are put in all spherical shells for immediate use on board ship?*

*A.*—The 5 second time fuze.

*Q.—How are the shells for riflea cannon fitted with fuzes?*

*A.*—One-half percussion, and one-half time.

*Q.—And the Parrott shells?*

*A.*—Are to have ten per cent. of rings for the Navy time fuze.

*Q.— What is the usual windage for shot and shells from smooth bore guns?*

*A.*—Fifteen hundredths of an inch; but when *shot* are fired from shell-guns, and *shells* from the XV-in. gun, they are to have a mean windage of two-tenths of an inch.

**Grape Shot.**

*Q.— What is a stand of grape-shot?*

*A.*—It is composed generally of nine shot, the combined weight of which together with the iron stand, is equal to a solid shot of the gun they are intended for.

*Q.—How are they put up?*

*A.*—In a canvass cover around the stem of the stand, which is secured at the top, quilted firmly with marline and painted.

*Q.—At what distance are grape shot available against men-of-war?*

*A.*—Their penetration is not sufficient generally beyond 150 yards.

*Q.—Against men when exposed?*

*A.*—At distances varying from 200 to 300 yards.

*Q.*—*Against light vessels, boats, or masses of men?*

*A.*—A single stand from heavy guns may be available at about 400 yards, and a double stand at 300 yards.

*Q.*—*How great is the dispersion of the balls?*
*A.*—About one-tenth the distance.

*Q.*—*Would you use a solid shot and stand of grape together?*
*A.*—No. It is very objectionable.

*Q.*—*Would you fire grape and canister together?*
*A.*—No. They cannot be fired together with any certainty of effect.

*Q.*—*What adds very much to the effect of either grape or canister?*
*A.*—A wad *behind* them.

### Canister.

*Q.*—*What are canister?*
*A.*—Iron or lead balls enclosed in a tin case, packed in sawdust, with both ends of the case closed.

*Q.*—*In what kind of guns are canister most used?*
*A.*—In the boat and field howitzers, and are effective against boats and bodies of men at short distances. They may be used also in any smooth bore gun.

### Shrapnel.

*Q.— What is a shrapnel?*

*A.*—A very thin shell filled with leaden or iron balls, consolidated by pouring in sulphur in a liquid state and allowing it to harden. A small cylindrical cavity is left from the fuze hole to the opposite surface of the shell which contains the bursting charge.

*Q.— What is the object of the shrapnel?*

*A.*—To extend the range of canister.

*Q.—How is this done.*

*A.*—The shell being fired from the gun remains intact until it reaches the desired distance when it is burst by the action of the fuze, and from that point the fragments of shell and the balls are dispersed like canister.

*Q.—The effect of a shrapnel then is the same as if a canister containing an equal number of balls and fragments was fired with a smaller charge from the same gun placed at the point where the shell exploded?*

*A.*—Yes.

*Q.— Why is only a small bursting charge put in the shrapnel?*

*A.*—In order that the balls and fragments may not be driven off too much laterally, but continue to move forward with the velocity imparted by the charge of the gun.

*Q.*—*In what cases then should shrapnel be used?*

*A.*—Only against masses of men fairly exposed, or but slightly covered by bushes or light framework.

*Q.*—*At what distance would you use shrapnel?*

*A.*—As a general rule at not less than 250 yards, and not more than 1000 yards. The Bormann fuze fitted to all shrapnel is intended to limit their application.

*Q.*—*At what distances from the point of bursting is the shrapnel effective?*

*A.*—For the small calibres not more than 250 yards. For the heavy guns double that distance.

## RIFLED CANNON AND PROJECTILES.

*Q.*— *What are the rifled cannon now in service?*

*A.*—The Parrott 150-pounder, 100-pounder, 60-pounder, 30-pounder, and 20-pounder; and the Dahlgren 20-pounder and 12-pounder—both the latter of bronze, and the former all of iron.

*Q.*— *What kinds of projectiles are fired from these guns?*

*A.*—From the heavy Parrott guns, those of his

own design; and also from the lesser calibres, the rifled projectiles of Hotchkiss and Schenkl. These are also fired from the Dahlgren guns, as well as their special projectiles.

*Q.— What kind of twist have these rifled guns ?*

*A.*—The Parrott an increasing twist, and the Dahlgren a regular twist.

*Q.— What charges of powder are intended for the Parrott guns ?*

*A.*—They are intended to use the charges of powder which a smooth bore gun of the same calibre would have with a round shot.

*Q.—And what weight of projectile ?*

*A.*—The projectiles are usually to be ten times that weight.

*Q.—Are projectiles of less than this full weight provided ?*

*A.*—Yes. In order to obtain greater initial velocity.

*Q.— What kind of powder is used in the Parrott guns ?*

*A.*—The common Navy cannon powder for the smaller calibres, and a larger grain for the 100 and 150-pounders.

*Q.— What do the projectiles for these rifled guns consist of ?*

*A.*—Of shells, shrapnel and solid shot—all elongated.

*Q.—Of what peculiar class are the rifled projectiles used in the Navy?*

*A.*—Of the expanding class, that is, forced into the grooves by the charge of the gun when fired.

*Q.—What precautions are taken in loading with them?*

*A.*—None other than with spherical, except that the base of every rifle projectile shall be greased before entering it into the gun; the grooves of the gun frequently cleaned from all residuum and dirt, and a moist sponge must also be invariably used.

*Q.—After firing what should be done?*

*A.*—Always *oil* the bore with a sponge.

*Q.—Is it neccessary that the projectile should be close "home?"*

*A.*—Most necessary, not only to avoid excess of strain upon the gun, but to ensure the projectile taking the grooves; otherwise it will tumble and fall short.

*Q.—How is the charge being "home" made certain?*

*A.*—By marking the rammer handle, as in the case of the smooth bores.

*Q.—In batteries of rifle guns on shore, what precautions should be taken in loading and firing?*

*A.*—To prevent dirt, sand or any foreign substances being carried into the bores on the sponge, projectile, or by the wind.

*Q.—How is this to be accomplished?*

*A.*—By using a canvass cover, wad, or tompion during the intervals of loading and firing, removing them just before discharging the gun.

*Q.—If it is found that the Parrott projectiles do not take the grooves, how may this be remedied?*

*A.*—By separating the brass ring a little, in several places, from the base of the shell.

*Q.—In the service of Parrott guns, what precaution is necessary in "running out" to port on board ship?*

*A.*—Not to start the shot from its seat, as being greased it slips down easily into the bore, and a slight shock when the bore is level will start the shot.

*Q.—How then must you avoid this, especially to leeward?*

*A.*—By elevating the gun and easing it out to port.

*Q.—Can spherical shot be used from these guns?*

*A.*—Yes, with excellent effect, especially in ricochet; the shot being first wrapped with felt or canvass.

*Q.—How is the vent made in the Parrott guns?*

*A.*—In a bouching of pure copper, screwed into

the gun. In the largest calibres its bottom is bouched with platinum.

*Q.—This copper being soft, how is its upper surface protected from the blow of the lock hammer?*

*A.*—By a piece of steel three-quarters of an inch thick, inserted over the copper.

*Q.— What kind of sights are fitted to the Parrott guns?*

*A*—Two, a breech sight and a front sight, the former movable in a socket secured to the rear of the wrought iron band, the latter fixed and screwed into the right rimbase.

*Q.— What additional arrangement has the breech sight?*

*A.*—A sliding eye-piece, capable of lateral adjustment to allow for the "drift" of the projectiles up to 10 degrees, and the effect of the wind across the line of fire.

*Q.—In what direction are these guns rifled?*

*A.*—To the *right*, that is, the projectile is made to turn from left to right, the observer standing at the breech of the gun.

*Q.— What is "drift?"*

*A.*—This is a deviation caused by the rifling, and in all guns is always in the direction of the twist, *when not influenced by the wind;* and must be allowed for in accurate firing.

*Q.—Suppose you are firing at long range, and the vessel moving across the line of fire, what is the result—give an example?*

*A.*—If the vessel was moving in that direction six knots, the gun elevated 15 degrees, and the time of flight 18 seconds, the deviation would be upwards of 60 yards.

*Q.—Have the heavy Navy Parrott guns much preponderance?*

*A.*—No. In order to obtain readily the changes of elevation.

*Q.—How are they elevated?*

*A.*—By means of a screw passing through a nut let through the neck of the cascabel.

*Q.—Is the heel of the screw confined, and why?*

*A.*—It is shackled to the rear transom in order to obtain the necessary purchase in moving the breech, as the gun has not much preponderance.

*Q.—What difficulty is experienced with these screws to the Parrott guns?*

*A.*—Having little preponderance, the breech moves violently when the gun is fired, and the screws, if not allowed sufficient play in the shackle at the heels, will sometimes break.

## SERVICE OF MAGAZINES.

*Q.— Who has the immediate charge of the magazines on board ship?*
*A.*—The Gunner and his mates.

*Q.— What is the first thing to be attended to before receiving powder into a magazine?*
*A.*—To see that it is thoroughly clean, well dried and ventilated, and that the lamps in the light-rooms, the magazine screens, dresses and shoes, the bilge cock and hose for flooding the magazine, and all the implements are in perfect order and ready for service, and that the cocks are accessible from the deck.

*Q.—How is the powder put up for use on board ship?*
*A.*—In cartridges of the specified weight for the different classes of guns on board, and stowed in copper tanks fitted with water-tight lids screwed down.

*Q.—How are these tanks stowed in the magazine?*
*A.*—On racks built for the purpose, with their lid ends out and hinges down.

*Q.—How are they distinguished so as to avoid mistakes in the proper cartridges?*
*A.*—Each tank is marked on the lid with the cal-

ibre and weight of the gun for which the cartridges are intended. The tanks containing musket powder are marked MUSKET POWDER, and those containing saluting powder are marked SALUTING.

*Q.—What is the regulation color for all cartridge bags containing service charges?*

*A.*—White; but when a deficiency of this color exists, the cartridges for all classes of guns may be distinguished by the colors of the bags, which must also be painted on the lid ends of the tanks.

*Q.—What are the colors used?*

*A.—White* for distant firing; *blue* for ordinary firing; *red* for near firing.

*Q.—When white alone is used, how are the charges distinguished?*

*A.*—The calibre and weight must be distinctly stencilled on each bag.

*Q.—Where are the tanks containing the charges for ordinary firing usually stowed?*

*A.*—Nearest the scuttles, for readier service.

*Q.—When tanks are emptied, where are they stowed?*

*A.*—On the upper shelves, so as to keep the powder as much as possible below the water line.

*Q.—Is loose powder ever taken, or carried on board a man-of-war?*

*A.*—No. And *all powder* must be stowed in the magazines.

*Q.*—*What articles for the service of the guns and small arms are positively prohibited from being in the magazines?*

*A.*—All articles containing fulminating matter, such as percussion and friction primers, percussion caps, and metallic cartridges for breech loading arms.

*Q.*—*Where are fireworks stowed?*

*A.*—On the racks in the magazine passage, in their proper boxes, after removing caps and primers, if the fireworks are made to be lighted by them.

*Q.*—*If powder is received on board in barrels, where are they to be unheaded?*

*A.*—The hoops and heads must be started on the orlop or berth deck; no coopering must ever be done in a ship's magazine.

*Q.*—*When a magazine is to be opened, what precautions are to be observed before entering?*

*A.*—Every precaution must be taken to guard against fire; all the men stationed in or about the magazine must put on the magazine dress and shoes, and put away everything metallic they may have about them.

*Q.*—*What are the regulations in regard to the ordinary fires and lights on board ship, when the magazines are opened?*

*A.*—All cooking fires, and all lights must be put out, except the light in the light room, the necessary lights on the lower deck for passing powder, and the dark lantern of the master-at-arms who attends the light rooms.

*Q.—How are the magazines of ships constructed generally?*

*A.*—They are made perfectly water-tight by caulking, then lined with boards inside, which are covered with sheet lead, including the floors.

*Q.—How are they lighted?*

*A.*—By means of one regulation lamp, to correspond with each alley of the magazine room, placed in a suitable box.

*Q.—How are they ventilated during action?*

*A.*—By providing grating hatches to admit of fresh air to the men; and to allow the dampness caused by perspiration to pass off.

*Q.—How are they flooded, when necessary to do so in case of fire on board of ship?*

*A.*—Each magazine is provided with an independent cock for filling it rapidly with water, with a waste pipe leading from the upper tier of tanks to carry off the superfluous water, and a cock just at the floor for letting off the water when the magazine is to be emptied after being flooded.

*Q.—How are the cocks to be turned?*

*A.*—From the deck above by means of a lever.

*Q.—How is the dampness of a magazine ascertained?*

*A.*—Dip a sponge in a solution of salt water, dry and weigh it, and hang it in the magazine; if it becomes heavier, the magazine is damp.

*Q.—State the capacities of the different powder tanks?*

*A.*—200 pounds, 150 pounds, 100 pounds, and 50 pounds.

*Q.—When receiving or landing powder, what is the usual signal hoisted?*

*A.*—The red flag at the fore, at the magazine on shore, and in the boats conveying the powder.

*Q.—What are the regulation shoes for magazines?*

*A.*—Wholly of buckskin or cotton canvas; india rubber or woolen are strictly forbidden.

*Q.—When the magazines are opened to supply powder, are the lids of the tanks immediately opened?*

*A.*—No. Not until orders are given to that effect, and then only of enough tanks to supply the charges ordered.

*Q.—Where are the keys of the magazines and their cocks kept?*

*A.*—Always in the captain's cabin.

*Q.—How is the powder in magazines prevented from caking?*

*A.*—By frequently turning the tanks over on their sides.

*Q.—Before closing the magazines what care should be taken?*

*A.*—To screw up the lids of the tanks, sweep carefully the floors and passages of all dirt and loose grains of powder, and put away in their proper places the dresses, shoes, passing boxes and implements. When closed and the hatches on, the keys are returned to the captain.

## PASSING POWDER.

*Q.—How is powder passed from the magazine to the guns?*

*A.*—In passing boxes, properly painted and marked for each class of gun. The full boxes are handed through scuttles cut through the decks.

*Q.—Does each description of gun require a separate chain of scuttles?*

*A.*—Yes. Unless the guns of another description have cartridges of the same diameter, weight and form.

*Q.—Give an example?*

A.—The VIII-in. of 63 cwt., and the 32-pounder of 57 cwt.

*Q.—In a frigate with two magazines, one forward and one aft, how are the guns supplied?*

A.—The forward half of the guns on each deck are supplied from the forward magazine, and the after half from the after magazine.

*Q.—How are the empty boxes returned below?*

A.—Through a canvas shoot at scuttles corresponding with those for the full boxes.

*Q.—How are cartridges delivered from the magazines?*

A.—They are passed up from them to the orlop, or berth deck, before they are put into the passing boxes.

*Q.—Are the boxes ever passed into the magazines during action or exercise?*

A.—No. Or even inside of the magazine screens.

*Q.—Where are they filled?*

A.—At the screen, but outside of it.

*Q.—How are passing boxes painted?*

A.—Black, with the calibre and charge in white letters, $2\frac{1}{2}$ inches long on the side, and $1\frac{1}{2}$ inches from the top.

*Q.—Suppose guns of same calibre on spar-decks require lighter charges?*

*A.*—The lower half of the boxes are painted *white*, and for gun-decks *red*.

*Q.—What is always done with empty passing boxes returned by the shoots?*

*A.*—They are landed on wet swabs; then turned upside down and struck over a fire-tub filled with water, having a wire grating cover.

*Q.—Why?*
*A.*—In order to free them from any loose fire.

## SHELL ROOMS.

*Q.—What preparations are necessary in the construction of shell-rooms?*

*A.*—Rooms for the stowage of loaded shells on board ship, should have the same care in construction and protection against an enemy's shot, and in provision for lighting and flooding as the magazines.

*Q.—How are the loaded shells stowed?*

*A.*—Each kind and calibre, and each length of fuze is to be stowed on separate tiers.

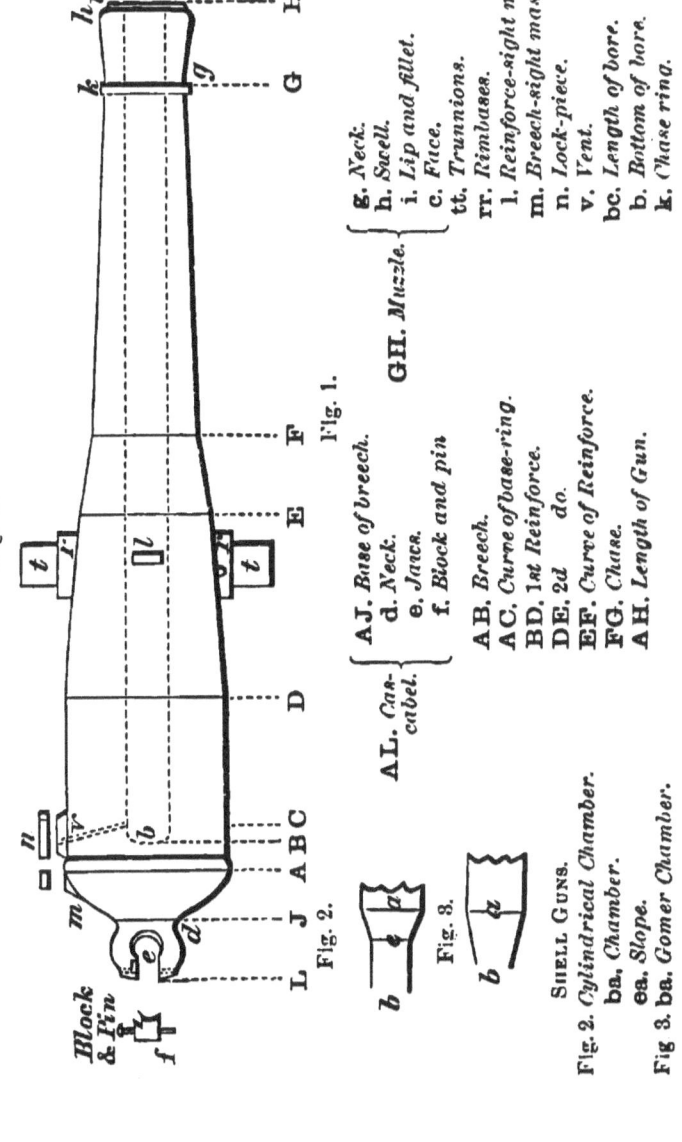

Fig. 1.

AL. Cascabel. { AJ. Base of breech.
d. Neck.
e. Jaws.
f. Block and pin

AB. Breech.
AC. Curve of base-ring.
BD. 1st Reinforce.
DE. 2d do.
EF. Curve of Reinforce.
FG. Chase.
AH. Length of Gun.

GH. Muzzle. { g. Neck.
h. Swell.
i. Lip and fillet.
c. Face.
tt. Trunnions.
rr. Rimbases.
l. Reinforce-sight mass.
m. Breech-sight mass.
n. Lock-piece.
v. Vent.
bc. Length of bore.
b. Bottom of bore.
k. Chase ring.

SHELL GUNS.
Fig. 2. Cylindrical Chamber.
ba, Chamber.
ea, Slope.
Fig. 3. ba. Gomer Chamber.

*Q.—Are empty shells stowed in the shell rooms?*

*A.*—No. They are to be stowed by themselves, unsabotted, in bulk in a dry place.

## GUNS AND CARRIAGES.

### I. Smooth Bores.

*Q.—Give the names of the different parts of the old pattern smooth bore guns?*

*A.*—1. The *cascabel,* which includes base of breech, neck, jaws, block and pin.
2. Breech.
3. Base ring and its curve.
4. 1st and 2d reinforce.
5. Curve of reinforce.
6. Chase and ring.
7. Muzzle, including the neck, swell, lip and fillet, and muzzle-face.
8. Trunnions.
9. Rimbases.
10. Lock piece.
11. Breech and reinforce sight masses.
12. Bore and vent.

*Q.—Name the different parts of the new model, or "Dahlgren" smooth bore guns?*

*A.*—1. The cascabel, which includes base of breech, neck, screwhole, jaws, block and pin.
2. Breech.
3. Base ring.
4. Cylinder.
5. Cone.
6. Chase.
7. Muzzle, including swell and muzzle face.
8. Trunnions.
9. Rimbases.
10. Locklugs.
11. Breech and front sight mass.
12. Bore, chamber and vent.

*Q.— What is called the length of a gun?*

*A.*—The distance from rear of base ring, along the axis of bore, to face of muzzle.

*Q.— What is the extreme length of a gun?*

*A.*—From the rear of cascabel, along the axis of bore to face of muzzle.

*Q.— What is meant by the calibre of a gun?*

*A.*—The diameter of its bore.

*Q.— What is the excess of weight in the breech of a gun called?*

*A.*—Preponderance.

*Q.— Why are guns made thicker at the breech?*

*A.*—In order to resist the effort of the charge, which is the greatest at that point.

*Q.— What is the usual dimensions of trunnions?*

*A.*—One calibre in length and diameter. In the new wrought iron carriages the length is diminished to suit the brackets.

*Q.—How are they always placed?*

*A.*—With their axis at right angles to that of the bore.

*Q.—If placed below the axis of bore?*

*A.*—Then they will break their carriages, owing to their irregular and violent movement in recoil.

*Q.— What are the usual forms of chambers in Navy guns?*

*A.*—In the Dahlgren guns the chambers are conical and designed to hold exactly the service charge; in the old patterns, they are bored with a slope towards the cylinder of the bore.

*Q.— What is the standard diameter of the vent?*

*A.*—Two-tenths of an inch.

*Q.— Where do guns commence to show signs of weakness in service?*

*A.*—Always at the lower orifice of the vent, where a crack will be seen after a certain number of rounds, and which will continue to widen and extend until the gun gives way.

*Q.—Can this be depended on, as a sign of weakness?*

*A.*—It can with certainty, and therefore, in service, impressions of the vent in wax, or in a composition of tallow, wax and charcoal, should be taken at least every twenty-five rounds.

*Q.—How are Navy guns designated?*

*A.*—As shot and shell guns—shot guns by the weight of the shot, as 32-pounder; and shell guns by the diameter of bore, as XI-in., IX-in., etc.

*Q.—What are the smooth-bore shot guns of the Navy?*

*A.*—32-pounders of 61, 57, 51, 46, 42, 33, and 27 cwt., and the 64-pounder of 106 cwt., the three last named being, however, nearly obsolete.

*Q.—Name the shell guns?*

*A.*—XV-in., XI-in., X-in., IX-in., and VIII-in. of 55 and 63 cwt.

*Q.—Are* shells *used from the 32-pounders?*

*A.*—Yes. They may be used, and are always supplied in certain proportions.

*Q.—Are* shot *ever used from the shell guns?*

*A.*—Yes. And are also supplied in certain proportions.

*Q.—What is the diameter of the bore of a 32-pounder?*

*A.*—6.4 inches.

# Naval Truck-Carriage.

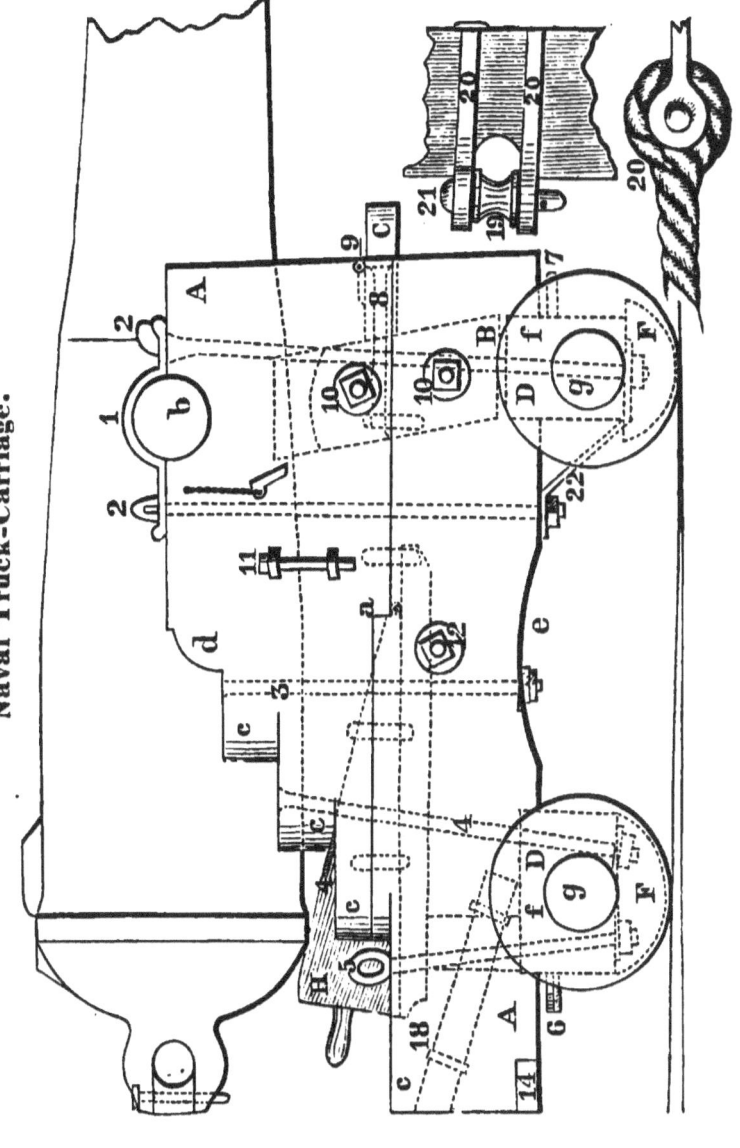

# Naval Truck-Carriage.

## Fig. 3.

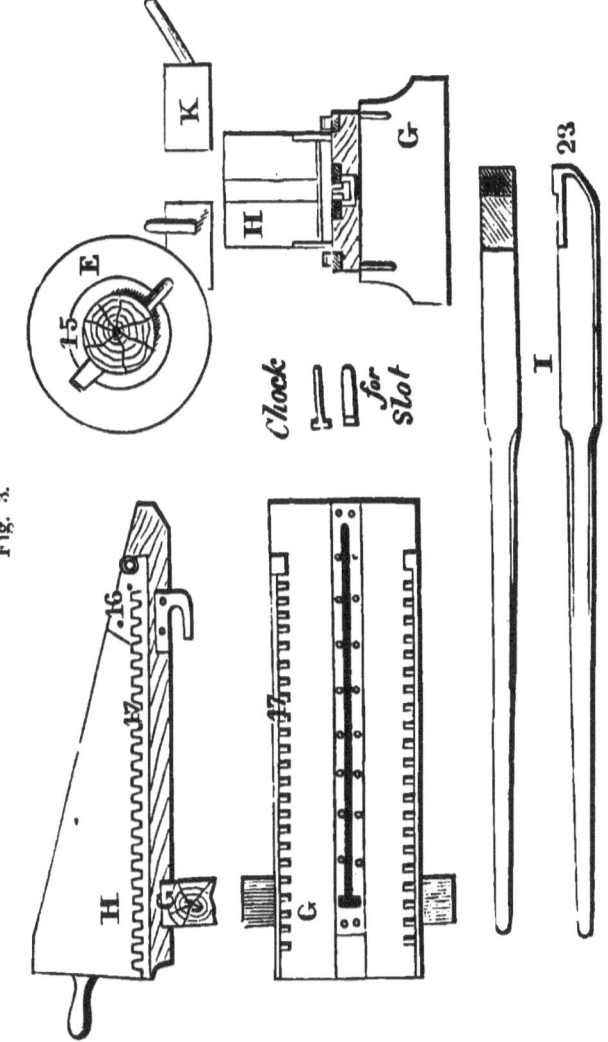

*Q.—What is the diameter of bore of the 64-pounder of* 106 *cwt.?*

*A.*—It is 8 inches, and its shot and shell weigh the same as the VIII-in. shell guns.

*Q.—How are these different guns generally mounted on board ship?*

*A.*—The 64-pounder and the XI-in. and X-in. are always mounted as pivot guns on slide carriages, and the rest, with the exception of the XV-in., are usually mounted on truck or Marsilly carriages in broadside.

*Q.—Name the different parts of the ordinary truck carriage for broadside?*

*A.*—1. Brackets.
2. Transoms.
3. Breast-piece.
4. Front and rear axletrees.
5. Front and rear trucks.
6. Dumb trucks.
7. Bed and stool.
8. Quoin.

*Q.—What are the implements?*

*A.*—Handspike, and chocking quoin.

*Q.—In what does the Marsilly carriage differ principally from the ordinary truck carriage?*

*A.*—In the Marsilly carriage there are no rear trucks, the lower piece of the brackets resting upon the deck to cause greater friction, and in place of the rear axle there is a rear transom, upon which is bolted a saucer for the heel of the elevating screw.

*Q.—Name the parts of the Marsilly carriage?*
*A.*—1. Brackets.
2. Front and rear transoms.
3. Breast piece.
4. Front axle.
5. Front trucks.
6. Elevating screw.

*Q.— What are the implements?*
*A.*—Roller and ordinary handspikes and chocking quoins.

*Q.— What other arrangement is there peculiar to these carriages, though not attached to them?*
*A.*—Sweep-pieces, fastened to the port sill, and fitted with hinges, to be thrown up out of the way when the gun is secured.

*Q.— What is the object of these sweep-pieces?*
*A.*—To facilitate training the gun in action.

*Q.—Of what is a pivot carriage principally composed?*
*A.*—Of a carriage and slide; the former moving upon the latter on metal trucks which are fitted to eccentric axles so as to be thrown in and out of action; and the latter resting upon training trucks upon the deck circles, and pivoted by means of a

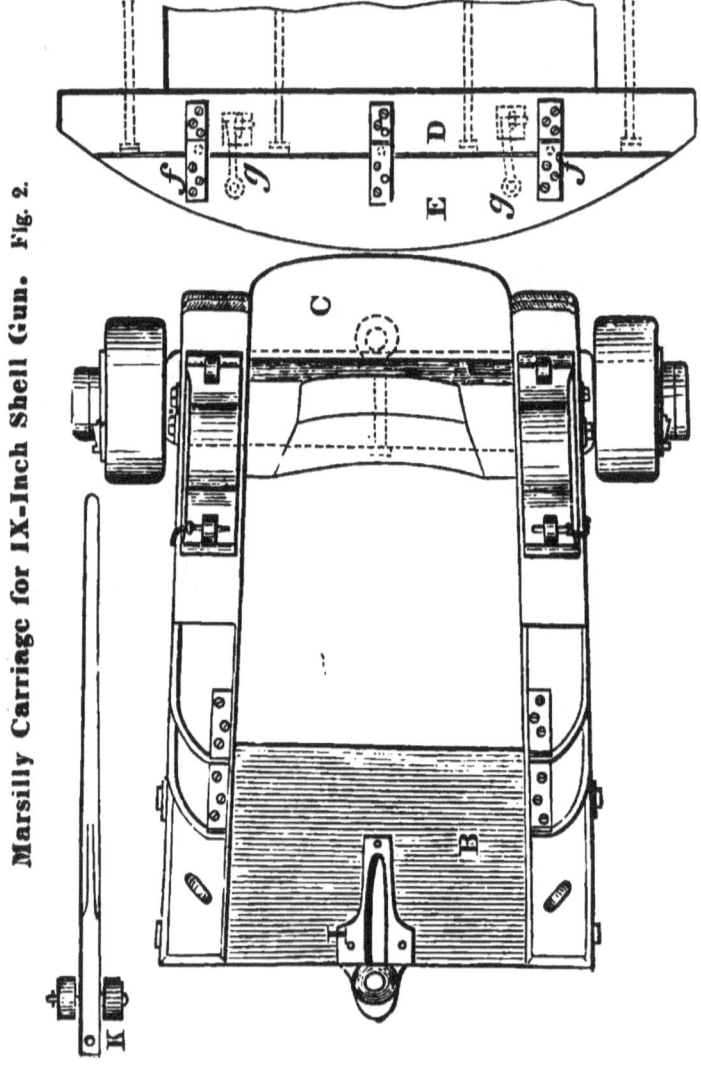

Marsilly Carriage for IX-Inch Shell Gun. Fig. 2.

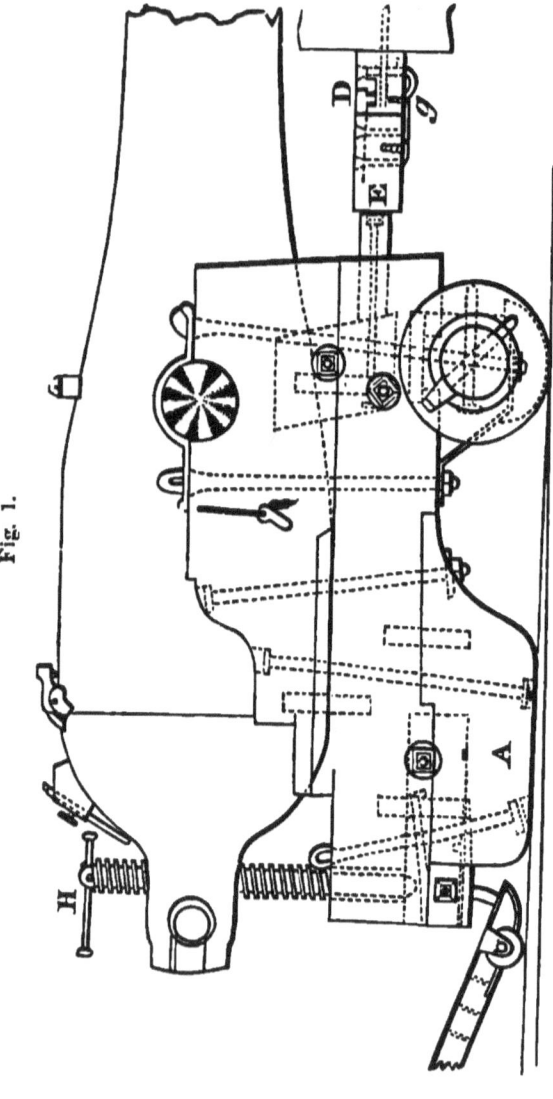

Marsilly Carriage for IX-Inch Shell Gun.

Fig. 1.

# Marsilly Carriage for IX-Inch Shell Gun.

NOMENCLATURE OF PARTS.

**A.** *The lowest piece of the Bracket, in place of rear truck of ordinary Carriage.*
**B.** *Rear Transom, in place of rear axle.*
**C.** *Breast-piece.*
**D. E.** *Sweep-pieces fixed.*
**D.** *Fixed below the Port-sill.*
**E.** *Movable, with brass catches (f.f.) and hooks and eyes (g. g.)*
**H.** *Elevating screw and lever, with saucer (I), in place of bed and quoin.*
**K.** *Roller Handspike.*
**L.** *Loop for Handspike.*

## Plan of XI-Inch Gun-Carriage and Slide.

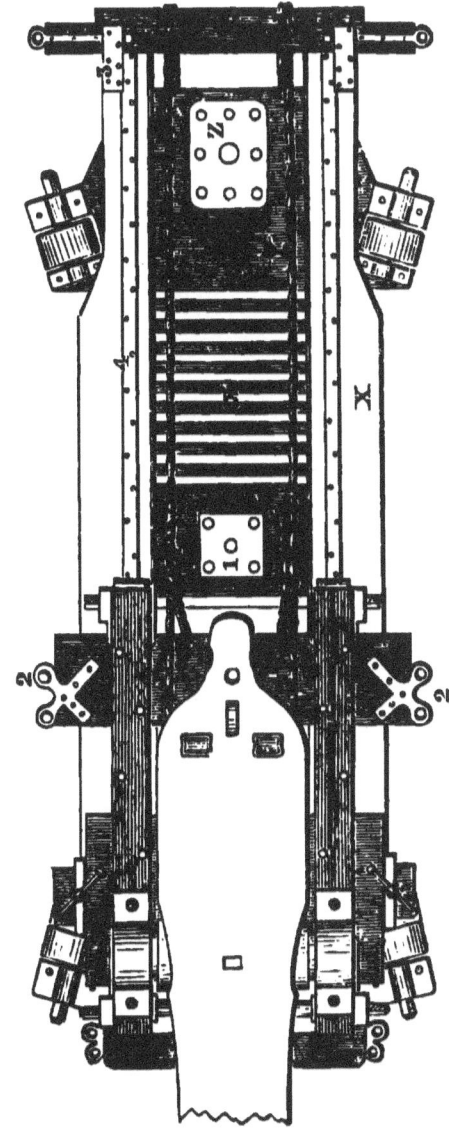

**Wooden Parts.**

X. *Battens and Slats.*
Y. *Preventer Breechings.*

**Metal Parts.**

Z. *Upper Pivot-plate.*
1. *Middle Roller-plate.*
2. *Eyes for Tackles.*
3. *Hurter Straps.*
4. *Rail Plates.*

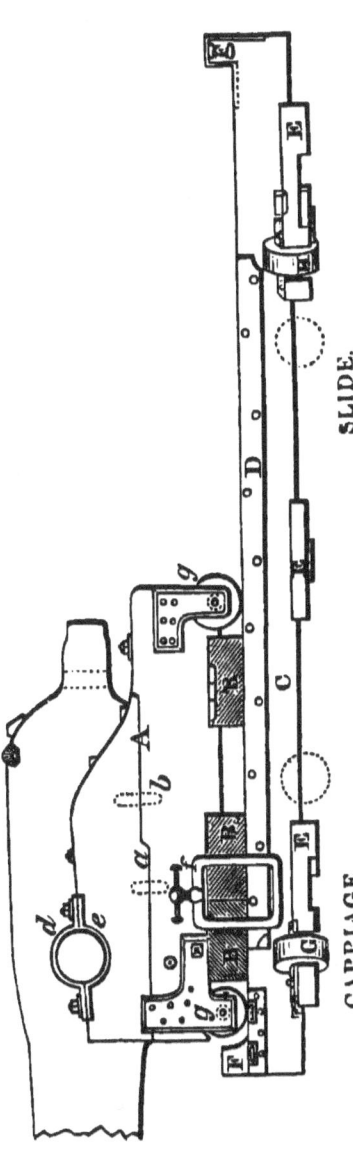

### CARRIAGE.

**WOODEN PARTS.**

- **A.** Brackets of two pieces, with jog (a.) and dowels (b.)
- **B.** Transoms, (projecting beyond the rails,) front, middle, and rear, jogged into brackets.

**METAL PARTS.**

- **d.** Cap squares
- **e.** Trunnion plates.
- **f.** Compressor, with screw and lever.
- **g.** Rollers and journal plates.

### SLIDE.

**WOODEN PARTS.**

- **C.** Rails.
- **D.** Compressor battens.
- **E.** Transoms; front and rear each in two parts, middle in one part.
- **F.** Hurters, front and rear.

**METAL PARTS.**

- **G.** Shifting trucks.
- **H.** Training trucks, both with journals and eccentric axles.

stout bolt let down through it and into a metal socket fitted in the deck.

*Q.—How is the recoil controlled?*

*A.*—By throwing the carriage trucks out of action, thus letting the transoms down on the slide, and by compressors which bind the forward transoms on each side to the slide.

*Q.—Name the parts of the carriage?*

*A.*—The wooden parts are:
1. Brackets.
2. Transoms—front, middle and rear.

The metal parts are:
1. Capsquares.
2. Trunnion plates.
3. Compressor with screw and lever.
4. Rollers and journal plates.

*Q.—Name the principal parts of the slide?*

*A.*—The wooden parts are:
1. Rails.
2. Compressor battens.
3. Transoms—front, middle and rear.
4. Hurters, front and rear.

The metal parts are:
1. Shifting trucks, journals, and eccentric axle.
2. Training trucks, journals, and eccentric axle.

*Q.—How much recoil is allowed to a broadside gun?*

*A.*—Sufficient to permit the muzzle to come in

far enough for easy loading—usually about 18 inches clear of the port.

## THE XV-INCH GUNS.

*Q.—For what particular vessels were these guns designed?*

*A.*—For the turrets of iron clad vessels.

*Q.—How are they mounted in the turrets?*

*A.*—Side by side, on iron compressor carriages specially adapted for them.

*Q.—Is the operation of tending the vent, sponging and loading, the same in these as in other guns?*

*A.*—They are the same with such modifications of the rammer and sponge as the close quarters of the turret render necessary; and the shot or shell is lifted to the muzzle by means of an elevator designed specially for the purpose.

*Q.—How is the gun pointed?*

*A.*—The elevation or depression is obtained by a spirit level attached to the gun and the direction of aim is given by the revolution of the turret by machinery.

*Q.— Who directs the pointing?*

*A.*—The captain, standing above in the pilot house.

*Q.—Is the firing confined to any particular direction?*

*A.*—No—but it is generally done in a line with the keel, the vessel always, if possible, fighting bows on.

*Q.—What is the charge of powder for the XV-in. guns?*

*A.*—35 and 50 pounds of ordinary cannon powder.

*Q.—What are the weights of the projectiles used in the XV-in guns?*

*A.*—Solid shot, 440 pounds.
Cored shot, 400 pounds.
Shell, 330 pounds.

*Q.—What is the charge for the XV-in. shell?*

*A.*—13 pounds.

*Q.—How is it fuzed?*

*A.*—With three of the Navy time fuzes, $3\frac{1}{2}$, 5, and 7 seconds.

*Q.—What precaution must be taken in loading with these shells?*

*A.*—The shell being very heavy, is apt to slip in the straps, therefore care must be taken to examine it well before pushing it down into the bore, because if one of the fuzes should be against the charge of powder in the gun, the shell would be broken and the gun injured.

*Q.— What rule is to be observed in using these shot and shell in action?*

*A.*—Not to throw any away. The *solid shot* should only be used against iron clads or masonry, with a charge of 50 pounds, and then only at distances where they will be surely effective.

*Q.— What elevation will the ports of a turret admit of?*

*A.*—8 degrees, extreme elevation.

*Q.—Are these guns available in ricochet firing?*

*A.*—No guns give a more regular and direct ricochet fire — the projectile bounding low, and *rolling* for a considerable distance on the water toward the end of its flight.

*Q.— Cannot grape, canister and shrapnel be used from these guns?*

*A.*—Yes. And in the same manner and for the same purposes as from other smooth bored cannon. They are furnished in certain proportions with every gun.

*Q.—Is there any danger of bursting to be apprehended in using such large guns?*

*A.*—Recent trials with the first gun of the class prove that they can be safely trusted to nearly 1000 rounds, certainly up to 600.

*Q.—Do the muzzles protrude beyond the turret?*

*A.*—The first guns made had their muzzles shortened so as to fire inside the turret. Those now being made have their muzzles long enough to project outside the turret.

*Q.—Is the shock of firing these guns in the turrets uncomfortable?*

*A.*—By no means, and not by any means so annoying as the shock from an enemy's shot.

*Q.—Is any useful effect to be expected in firing shells from the XV-in. gun with charges above 35 pounds cannon powder?*

*A.*—No. Except in cases where the shell will not reach the object without increasing the charge above 35 pounds.

*Q.— What is the maximum charge which can be burnt in the XV-in. gun with a shell?*

*A.*—Fifty pounds cannon powder.

*Q.— When should cored shot be used from the XV-in. gun?*

*A.*—Only against masonry at short range, and then with charges of 50 pounds.

*Q.— What precaution is to be taken in loading with cored shot?*

*A.*—That the *plug of the core hole is outward in the bore?*

*Q.—At close quarters, when firing with solid shot, what increased charge can be used from the XV-in. guns, and how many?*

*A.*—Sixty pounds may be used for twenty rounds at from 50 to 150 yards.

*Q.—In loading with the shell fitted with three fuzes, how would you arrange them?*

*A.*—When the distance is known to be *less* than the range of the *shortest* fuze, and time will admit of doing so, *uncap all the fuzes*. At other times uncap the fuze suited to the distance, and the one of longest time of burning.

## MORTARS AND MORTAR PRACTICE.

*Q.—What kinds of mortars are used at sea?*

*A.*—There are two kinds; one secured to the bed by trunnions placed near the breech, the other by a plate cast upon the breech.

*Q.—Which of the two kinds is now used in the Navy?*

*A.*—The trunnion mortar.

*Q.—What is its calibre and weight?*

*A.*—13 inches, and 17,200 pounds.

*Q.—For what particular service are they intended?*

*A.*—For bombardment—that is, throwing shells at high elevation into towns, cities, and fortifications.

*Q.—How is the trunnion mortar set at any desired angle?*

*A.*—By means of a quoin or wedge under the muzzle.

*Q.— When has it the greatest range?*

*A.*—At from 35 to 45 degrees.

*Q.— When is the range reduced?*

*A.*—Below 35 and above 45 degrees.

*Q.—At which angle is it usual to fix the mortar?*

*A.*—At 45 degrees, in order to get the greatest *fall* of shell.

*Q.—How is the range then reduced?*

*A.*—By decreasing the charge.

*Q.—Suppose you wish a very short range?*

*A.*—Then increase the angle to 60 degrees. This answers the purpose without decreasing the *fall* of the shell.

*Q.— When should a mortar mounted on board ship be fired?*

*A.*—Only when the deck is level.

*Q.— Why is it so necessary in mounting mortars on board ship to shore up the decks, and otherwise strengthen them and the hull?*

*A.*—Not only to support the heavy weight of mortar and bed, but because the mortar has *no recoil.*

*Q.—How are the full service charges for mortars put up?*

*A.*—In white cotton bags, and are passed from the magazine in leather passing boxes.

*Q.—In the service of magazines on board mortar vessels, what precautions are necessary?*

*A.*—Large tubs of water must be placed near the magazines, with buckets at hand, and wet swabs to cut off trains of powder.

*Q.—Suppose the object to be assaulted is a large one, cannot the position be fixed by judging the distance, and without the sextant?*

*A.*—Yes. After two or three bombs have been fired.

*Q.— When a vessel, having obtained her position, is obliged to move out of the line of battle, what should be done?*

*A.*—A small buoy should be dropped under foot to mark her position, with her name or number marked upon it.

*Q.—How is the true direction of fire obtained on board ship with a mortar?*

*A.*—By the trunnion sights, and a white line painted on the mortar bed, parallel to axis of bore when level.

*Q.—How is the mortar pointed on shore?*

*A.*—Determine practically two fixed points, in a line with the piece and the object—cover these with a plummet, and this gives the vertical plane, including the line of metal, which becomes the plane of fire.

*Q.—How may the distance be estimated by the bursting of the bomb?*

*A.*—Multiply the number of seconds which elapse between seeing the flash and the sound of the report from the bomb by 1100, and the product is nearly the distance in feet.

*Q.—Is this rule to be applied in action, and by whom?*

*A.*—Yes. By the officer in charge of the mortar, who also notes when a bomb *fails* to burst.

*Q.—How is the mortar vessel prepared for action?*

*A.*—Cover up fore rigging on side where mortar is to be used, send down foretopmast, unbend foresail, lay its boom and gaff on deck, lash rigging close into foremast, get spring on cable, lower the boats from side davits, cover all hatches with tarpaulins, and thoroughly wet the head sails.

*Q.—When are precautions against fire to be especially taken?*

*A.*—When firing against the wind, as then the flame from the mortar is thrown back inboard.

*Q.—What else must be done before going into action?*

. *A.*—Keep the broadside guns in readiness, and have muskets at hand and loaded to repel attack from enemy's boats.

*Q.—How is the bomb whipped up and lowered in the mortar?*

*A.*—By a gun-tackle purchase, rigged directly over it.

*Q.—Before firing what precaution is necessary with the mortar carriage?*

*A.*—That the eccentrics are thrown out of gear, and the circle flat upon the platform on which it revolves.

*Q.—When ranges are desired with reduced charges, where are they to be filled?*

*A.*—Always in the magazine, *never* anywhere else.

*Q.—Is it necessary to be exact in filling the charges for mortar firing?*

*A.*—Yes. Because an ounce of powder makes considerable variation in their range.

*Q.—Describe the manner of filling bombs?*

*A.*—First; see that they are quite clean and dry; then place them on a block made for the purpose, or on grommets of rope, or on the deck, eyes up; measure the charge carefully, and pour it in through a copper funnel.

*Q.—How is the fuze prepared?*

*A.*—Being driven in a wooden case, it is placed in a groove and sawed across at the proper length. It is then tried in the hole, and should enter three-quarters of its length, if not, it must be reduced by rasping.

*Q.—How is it driven to its place in the bomb?*

*A.*—Cover the head with tow to prevent breaking the composition, place the fuze setter on and drive it in with a mallet until the head is about two-tenths of an inch above the bomb.

*Q.— Who fills the bombs?*

*A.*—The Gunner, with two assistants.

*Q.— What is the most convenient place for cutting or preparing fuzes on board vessels?*

*A.*—The forward part above decks, under a heavy tent, to protect the fuzes from fire or rain.

*Q.—Is anything else ever used in bombs besides fuzes to ignite them?*

*A.*—Yes. They are sometimes fired with a piece of port-fire stuck into the fuze hole, which is a certain way of setting fire to buildings.

*Q.—Are any other projectiles ever fired from mortars besides bombs, or shells?*

*A.*—Yes. Carcasses containing inflamable mixtures, bags containing one pound balls, or ordinary grape shot, with very reduced charges and a wad placed between the powder and balls.

*Q.—How far will one pound of powder throw a 200 pound bomb?*

*A.*—About 300 yards.

### Implements for Service of Mortars.

The implements are arranged as follows:

HANDSPIKES.—Two on each side of the bed against

the cheeks, leaning upon the manœuvring bolts, the ends toward the vessel's sides, and those of the front handspikes even with the front of the cheeks.

HAVERSACK.—Containing fuzes, and a pair of sleeves, attached to the tompion.

TUBE POUCH.—Containing the priming wire, friction tubes, and lanyard, attached to the tompion, and lying on the mortar.

GUNNER'S POUCH.—Containing gunner's level, gimlet, vent punch and chalk, attached to tompion.

QUADRANT, PLUMMET, SCRAPER, WIPER, SHELL HOOKS.—In a basket between the cheeks of the mortar bed.

TOMPION.—In the muzzle.

QUOIN.—Under the mortar upon the bolster, with handle to the left.

MAUL, WRENCH, PINCERS, BROOM.—With the basket.

### Stations at Mortars.

No. 1. Captain attends and gives general orders about loading; points; inserts friction tube, and fires.

No. 2. Sponger and trainer.

No. 3. Loader and trainer.

No. 4. Shellman and trainer.

No. 5. Shellman and trainer.

No. 6. Handspike and train-tackle.

No. 7. Handspike and train-tackle.

No. 8. Eccentric bars.
No. 9. Eccentric bars.

When the eccentrics are raised, the bar is lashed down until the bomb is pointed at the object.

No. 10. In charge of quadrant and level line.
No. 11. Powderman.
No. 12. Officer in charge.
No. 13. To carry fuzes.
No. 14. To arrange fuze for distance.

### Mortar Exercise.

#### ORDERS.

#### 1. "*Prepare the Mortar.*"

At this order, No. 2 takes out the tompion and lays it in the rear, together with the implements. The train-tackles are manned; one leading aft, the other forward on the opposite side. The men at the eccentrics prepare to raise the circle off the bed, cast down the bars and go to train-tackles.

#### 2. "*Train.*"

The mortar is trained toward the side where it is to be served.

#### 3. "*Take Implements.*"

The gunner hands No. 3 the sleeves and wiper; to No. 2, the tube pouch and broom and to No. 4, the haversack; equips himself with the gunner's pouch, and applies the level to ascertain the line of metal, which he marks with chalk. The rear handspikemen place the handspikes under the rear of the mortar, to help the circle round the training. The word "halt!" is to be given when the piece is in the proper direction, and all resume their places.

### 4. "*Load by Detail.*"

The gunner, taking the scraper, places himself in front of the muzzle, and scrapes the bore and chamber; draws out the scrapings with the spoon, puts the scraper back in the basket, and again posts himself at the muzzle, one yard to the front.

The sponger, No. 2, takes the wiper in his right hand, faces to the left, with left foot near the manœuvring bolt, the right in front of the muzzle; the left hand upon the face of the piece; wipes out the mortar with the cartridge bag, and then uses the sponge to thoroughly cleanse the chamber and bore. As soon as this operation is performed, the captain of the piece clears the vent with the priming wire, sweeps the platform, and resumes his post.

The powderman goes to the rear for the cartridge, and, at the order "load!" the powder is to be carefully emptied into the chamber, without spilling on deck.

The two shellmen taking the handspike at each end, and small shell hooks, prepare to receive the shell from the hatch when it is whipped up. When the bomb is landed on deck, the hooks are to be inserted to the ears, and the handspike passed through the hook rings. In carrying the bomb, they hold the handspike by the right hands, moving to the left of the piece between the gunner and the muzzle, and resting the bomb upon the circle against the middle of the transom.

The shellmen raise the bomb from the deck, while No. 2 wipes it clean; the train-tacklemen seize on to the purchase, and whip up the bomb above the muzzle, and lower it carefully into the mortar—the powder being previously leveled off,—and the gunner adjusting the bomb, so that the fuze will be in the axis of the piece, unhooks and throws the hooks to the rear. At the same time, if wooden fuzes are used, he *uncaps* the fuze, holding up the cap, that the officer in charge may see it.

### 5. "*Elevate.*"

The gunner takes the quadrant from the basket, and applies it to the left side of the face of the mortar, with the left hand; then inserts or draws out the quoin with the right, giving the command "raise!" or "lower!" until the proper elevation is attained—usually 45 degrees; and returns the quadrant to the basket.

The officer in charge, or the gunner, gives the order "mortar right!" or "mortar left!" when the piece is pointed by the trunnion sights or other expedients, until the proper direction is obtained.

### 6. "*Prime.*"

The captain inserts the friction tube; the crew fall back in the rear; the officer in charge goes to a place where he can observe the effect of the bomb, ready to note in a book whether it falls to the right or left, too far or too short; the book to be ruled in proper form to prevent mistakes.

### 7. "*Fire.*"

The captain of the piece moves three paces to the rear, in a line with the right cheek, facing to the front, holding the toggle of the lanyard with his right hand, the lanyard *lightly* stretched, with the cord between the fingers, and breaks to the rear a full pace with the left foot, the left hand against the thigh.*

At the discharge of the mortar, the crew resume their stations, taking care at the moment of explosion to open their mouths, and *not* to stop their ears with their fingers.

### 8. "*Cease firing or exercise.*"

The order is given by the officer in charge, "Out of Battery!" when the piece is to be secured fore and aft to the circle by lashings, the implements placed as before the exercise, and the mortar covered with a canvas cover.

---

* In priming mortars by means of the friction tube, the lanyard should be passed under a rope attached to and tautly drawn between the rear manœuvring bolts.

## TABLES OF CHARGES, ELEVATIONS, AND RANGES FOR 13-INCH MORTARS.

*Charges for 13-inch Mortar Bombs.*

| CHARGE. | 13-INCH. | |
|---|---|---|
| | *lbs.* | *oz.* |
| Of shell filled........................................ | 11 | 0 |
| To burst shell....................................... | 6 | 0 |
| To blow out fuze.................................... | 0 | 6 |
| Ordinary service charge........................... | 7 | 0 |
| Incendiary, match, or other composition........... | 0 | 8 |

*Ranges with Sea Coast 13-inch Mortars, 20 degrees elevation.*

| CHARGE. | MEAN TIME OF FLIGHT. | LEAST RANGE. | GREATEST RANGE. | MEAN RANGE. |
|---|---|---|---|---|
| *Lbs.* | *Seconds.* | *Yards.* | *Yards.* | *Yards.* |
| 4 | 8 | 840 | 877 | 869 |
| 6 | 9.5 | 1209 | 1317 | 1263 |
| 8 | 11.66 | 1653 | 1840 | 1744 |
| 10 | 12.50 | 2010 | 2128 | 2066 |
| 12 | 14.25 | 2369 | 2688 | 2528 |
| 14 | 15.25 | 2664 | 2780 | 2722 |

*Ranges with 13-inch Mortars, at 45 degrees elevation.*

| CHARGE. | | FLIGHT. | FUZE. | | RANGE. |
|---|---|---|---|---|---|
| *Lbs.* | *oz.* | *Seconds.* | *Inches.* | *10ths.* | *Yards.* |
| 7 | | 21.4 | 4 | 2⅔ | 2190 |
| 7 | 8 | 22.4 | 4 | 4 | 2346 |
| 8 | | 23.2 | 4 | 6 | 2480 |
| 8 | 8 | 23.8 | 4 | 7½ | 2600 |
| 9 | | 24.4 | 4 | 8¾ | 2734 |
| 9 | 8 | 24.9 | 4 | 9¾ | 2853 |
| 10 | | 25.4 | 5 | 1 | 2958 |
| 10 | 8 | 25.9 | 5 | 1¾ | 3026 |
| 11 | | 26.3 | 5 | 2½ | 3150 |
| 11 | 8 | 26.7 | 5 | 3½ | 3246 |
| 12 | | 27.0 | 5 | 4 | 3327 |
| 12 | 8 | 27.4 | 5 | 4¾ | 3404 |
| 13 | | 27.7 | 5 | 5½ | 3470 |
| 13 | 8 | 28.0 | 5 | 6 | 3552 |
| 14 | | 28.3 | 5 | 6½ | 3617 |
| 14 | 8 | 28.5 | 5 | 7 | 3681 |
| 15 | | 29.0 | 5 | 8 | 3739 |
| 15 | 8 | 29.1 | 5 | 8¼ | 3797 |
| 16 | | 29.2 | 5 | 8½ | 3849 |
| 16 | 8 | 29.4 | 5 | 8¾ | 3901 |
| 17 | | 29.6 | 5 | 9 | 3949 |
| 17 | 8 | 29.8 | 5 | 9½ | 3997 |
| 18 | | 29.8 | 5 | 9¾ | 4040 |
| 18 | 8 | 30.0 | 6 | | 4085 |
| 19 | | 30.2 | 6 | 0¼ | 4123 |
| 19 | 8 | 30.3 | 6 | 0½ | 4160 |
| 20 | | 30.5 | 6 | 1 | 4200 |

## BOAT GUNS, AND EXERCISE.

*Q.— What are the boat guns of the Navy?*

*A.*—The 12-pounder and 24-pounder smooth bore, and the rifled 12-pounder howitzer designed by Admiral Dahlgren.

*Q.— Of what are they made?*

*A.*—Of bronze, and are cast solid and bored out.

*Q.—Name the parts of the howitzer?*

*A.*—1. The cascabel, including the breech-plate, knob and neck.
  2. Base ring.
  3. Cylinder.
  4. Chase.
  5. Loop, with hole for bolt.
  6. Locklugs.
  7. Front sight on muzzle.
  8. Breech sight.
  9. Bore and chamber.
  10. Vent.

*Q.—How are these guns mounted?*

*A.*—On boat and field carriages for the 12-pounders, smooth and rifled, and on boat or deck carriages for the 24-pounders.

*Q.—Are the 12-pounders ever mounted on deck carriages?*

*A.*—Yes. In special cases, on the decks of light vessels.

*Q.—Name the parts of the boat carriage?*

*A.*—Bed, slide, compressor plate, compressor bolts and handles, and lugs for loop.

*Q.—Name the parts of the field carriage?*

*A.*—Axle, trail, braces, supports for transporting boxes, lugs for loop, trail wheel and bolt, socket for handspike, elevator—with disc and box.

*Q.—What are the weights of the bronze howitzers?*

*A.*—The 24-pounder, 1,300 pounds.
The 12-pounder, smooth, 760 pounds.
The 12-pounder, rifled, 880 pounds.

*Q.—What are the projectiles used with the smooth bores?*

*A.*—Shells, shrapnel, and canister.

*Q.—With the rifles?*

*A.*—Shot and shells.

*Q.—What are the service charges, and how are they put up?*

*A.*—For the 24-pounder, 2 pounds.
For the 12-pounder, 1 pound.
For the 12-pounder, rifle, 1 pound, and are always put up as "fixed ammunition," that is, the charges

attached to the sabots, except for the 12-pounder rifle, which has no sabot.

*Q.—Is there not also a light 12-pounder howitzer in service ?*

*A.*—Yes. There are a few weighing 430 pounds, but their manufacture is discontinued, except in special cases.

### Exercise of the Boat Howitzer.

*Q.—State generally the preparations for embarking the howitzer ?*

*A.*—While the boats are being cleared out, the officer of the boat sees the howitzer and its equipments got in readiness. The officer of the piece will attend to the gun and carriages, and the quarter-gunner gets up ammunition from below, and attends to supplying lock, sights, sponges, spare fuzes, pouches, primers, etc.

*Q.— Who examines in person the shrapnel and shells ?*

*A.*—The officer who is to command the boat.

*Q.— What are the duties of the captain of the gun ?*

*A.*—He looks after the traverses, trucks, pivot plates, etc.

*Q.— What are the duties of the coxswain of the boat ?*

*A.*—To have ready the thwarts, oars, masts, sails, etc.

*Q.*—*The boat being now ready for hoisting out, what should be done?*

*A.*—Lay thwarts and traverses, bolt pivot plates on bows and quarters; and if the *field* carriage is to go in the boat, lay the wheel and trail tracks.

*Q.*—*Suppose the stem and stern pivot plates interfere with the purchases for hoisting out the boats?*

*A.*—They can be secured after the boat is in the water.

*Q.*—*What is the general rule for hoisting the gun into the boat?*

*A.*—It should not be handled separately from one of its carriages, and may be hoisted in on either the boat or field carriage.

*Q.*—*Suppose the boat carriage is preferred?*

*A.*—Sling it with a stout strap passed through the loop-lugs and brought up round the gun, the carriage having been secured by the compressors a little towards rear end of slide in order to make the gun hang square.

*Q.*—*In a seaway, cannot the gun and carriage be hoisted out in the launch?*

*A.*—Yes. And then the carriage should be laid athwartships, with the two ends bolted into the bow pivot plates.

*Q.*—*What are the general arrangements in placing the gun, ammunition, etc., in the boat?*

*A.*—1. The gun may be in the bow on its boat carriage bolted to the stern pivot.

2. Field carriage aft with trail over quarter rail.

3. Ammunition in stern sheets, or elsewhere according to trim of boat, and its preservation from injury.

4. Captain of howitzer slings his haversack, having in it a supply of primers, a vent bit and vent cloth.

*Q.—Do Nos. 1 and 2 assist at the oars?*

*A.*—No. As the bow oars cannot be conveniently pulled with the howitzer in the bows.

*Q.— With a crew of 20 men, give the stations and duties in the boat and at the gun?*

*A.*—*Quarter-master*—stern sheets, signals and assists with ammunition.

*Quarter-gunner*—ammunition.

*Coxswain*—tends helm.

*Chief of piece*—in bows, superintends firing.

No. 1—starboard, bow oar. Is *Captain* of gun, points, fires, superintends orders, and orders in absence of officer.

No. 2—port bow oar, is 2d *Captain*, tends vent and primes.

No. 3—starboard, 2d oar, *sponger*, sponges and rams home charge.

No. 4—port, 2d oar, is *loader*, receives and enters ammunition.

No. 5—starboard, 3d oar, tends forward compressor.

No. 6—port, 3d oar, tends after compressor.

No. 7—starboard, 4th oar, train rope.

From No. 8 to 16, inclusive, man the starboard and port oars.

No. 17—starboard, 9th oar, and

No. 18—port, 9th oar, run field carriage forward when landing.

*Q.— Who directs the whole ?*

*A.*—The officer of the launch, or he may take special charge of the howitzer.

*Q.— What are the words of command ?*

*A*—Man the howitzer! (preliminary.)

1. Sponge!
2. Load!
3. Point!
4. Fire!

*Q.— What is done at the preliminary order, "Man the howitzer ?"*

*A.*—Captain of gun sees elevator, sight and lock are in order for firing.

Nos. 1, 2, 3, 4, 5, 6, 7 trail oars.

No. 3 goes to starboard side of muzzle, with sponge and rammer.

No. 4, to port side of muzzle, and takes out tompion.

No. 5, starboard side, near the forward compressor.

No. 6, port side, near after compressor.
No. 7, after end of slide, and hooks training rope.
No. 8, tends vent, and puts in primer.
If the gun is not loaded, it must be run in.

*Q.—At the order " sponge !" state the duties ?*

*A.*—No. 2 closes vent.

No. 3 enters sponge, presses it firmly to bottom of bore, turns it round and withdraws it.

Quarter-gunner takes a round from the ammunition box, and if shell or shrapnel be used, holds it for the officer in charge of the gun to adjust the fuze.

*Q.—At the word " load ?"*

*A.*—Quarter-gunner passes forward with the charge to the gun, covering it with his jacket to protect it.

No. 4 receives it from quarter-gunner, and enters it in bore.

No. 3 rams home to mark on rammer handle.

No. 2 puts in primer and covers it with his hand until Nos. 3 and 4 are clear of the gun.

*Q.—At the third command, "point ?"*

*A.*—Nos. 5 and 6 ease compressors.

All six numbers and captain of gun run out howitzer.

Nos. 5, 6 tauten compressors.

Officer of gun puts up sight as directed by officer of boat.

Captain of gun brings the elevation within limits of the boat's motion.

No. 7 trains nearly to object if the boat is under way.

*Q.—At the fourth command, "fire!" how is the operation performed?*

*A.*—Coxswain gives the helm a slight motion so as to sweep the gun sideways and across the object. Captain of gun watches this movement, keeping his eye close down on the sights, and draws the lock-laniard as soon as the sights bear on the object.

*Q.—After firing, what does the captain of the gun do?*

*A.*—He immediately coils up lock-laniard, and pulls from the vent any pieces of quill that remain in it, enters the bit to clear it entirely through.

*Q.—State briefly the precautions to be taken in sponging, loading, and firing the boat howitzer?*

*A.*—1. Keep vent closed in sponging.

2. Always use a moist sponge.

3. Be careful to guard the head of the fuze composition from the moisture of the fingers, rain, or the spray of the sea.

4. Never strike the ammunition in ramming home.

5. No. 2 should in ramming home, always keep his body at the side of the chase, *never* before the muzzle.

6. If the primer fails to fire the gun, take care not to approach it too soon; but after waiting a

little while, captain removes the broken primer, enters his boring bit down through the vent, and puts in a new primer.

*Q.—Is it necessary to prick the cartridge?*

*A.*—No. The primers have force enough to fire the charge without.

*Q.—What care is to be taken in compressing?*

*A.*—Not to force the compressors hard, a turn is generally sufficient.

*Q.—Should care be taken in tightening the thumb-screw of the sight?*

*A.*—Yes. It should not be forced, because it may soon strip the threads.

*Q.—If the primer fails on account of not drawing the lock-laniard properly?*

*A.*—If the wafer of the primer does not flash, No. 2 throws the lock back for a second trial.

### Pivoting the Howitzer.

*Q.—How much sweep is allowed by the stern pivot?*

*A.*—About one point and a-half, starboard and port.

*Q.—If this should not be enough, and it is inconvenient to move the boat?*

*A.*—Then the bow pivots must be used.

*Q.—What is the order to do this?*

A.—Pivot on the port (or starboard,) bow.

*Q.—Explain the operation?*

A.—No. 7, assisted by the other numbers, trains rear end of slide into bow pivot, which is *not* to be used.

No. 2 bolts it in.

No. 3 draws bolt out of stern pivot, and moves round forward end of slide into the pivot which is *to be used*, and drops in the bolt.

No. 2 then draws bolt from rear end of slide.

*Q.—How much of a sweep is included on the bow pivots?*

A.—An arc of about 120 degrees.

*Q.—How far abaft the beam is it advisable to train the howitzer when firing it on the bow pivots?*

A.—Not more than one point.

*Q.—Why?*

A.—Because the accidental explosion of a shell or shrapnel near the muzzle would be dangerous to those in the boat.

*Q.—If on the stern pivots?*

A.—Not more than one point forward of the beam, and for the same reason.

### Shifting the Howitzer.

*Q.— With the light 12-pounders, how may this be done?*

*A.*—As these, with their boat carriages, weigh about 660 pounds, they can easily be transported by hand from one end of the boat to the other.

*Q.— With the 24-pounder and heavy 12-pounder?*

*A.*—By placing rollers on the tracks laid for the field carriages, and using a light fall at each end of the carriage to keep it in command.

### Landing the Howitzer.

*Q.—In this operation, what are the words of command?*

*A.*—1. Prepare to land!
2. Trail!
3. Shift howitzer!
4. Land!

*Q.—At the first order, what is done?*

*A.*—Quarter-gunner fills pouches with one round each, passes them to the men, excepting Nos. 1 and 3. The men sling pouches over right shoulder, buckling the strap short, so as to keep the ammunition out of the water. Captain of gun also shortens strap of his haversack; the bow and stroke oars are trailed.

Nos. 1 and 2 adjust bed of boat carriage on slide

for shipping, place muzzle-block, and bear the muzzle on it by the elevator; pass strap round neck of cascabel; put shifting spar through strap. Quarter-gunner, assisted by men from the after oars, raises field carriage up on trucks.

*Q.—The second command, trail?*

*A.*—As soon as the boat is beached the men trail oars and jump to stations. Nos. 3 and 4 over bows to adjust skids.

Nos. 5, 6 launch skids.

No. 2 tends elevator.

No. 3 tends muzzle.

Nos. 8, 10, 11, 13 work shifting spar, helped by as many of the men as can get hold.

No. 7 draws loop bolt.

The stroke oarsmen run the field carriage forward, quarter-gunner guiding it on track by the trail.

*Q.—At the third command, "shift howitzer?"*

*A.*—Nos. 1, 2 clear elevator.

Heave up breech of gun by spar.

Nos. 5, 6 back the bed on slide.

Run field carriage forward until its lugs come under loop of howitzer.

Lower the piece.

Put in loop bolt and elevator; hook on drag rope, and ship trail handspike in socket.

*Q.—Explain the operations at the fourth command, "land?"*

*A.*—Nos. 5, 6, 7, 8 jump out of boat, and with

Nos. 3, 4 divide to each skid, keeping *outside* of them.

Stroke oarsmen wheel the piece up to gunwale by the spokes, the quarter-gunner guiding the trail by the handspike; rest of crew take hold of drag rope to ease gun down from the bow, the quarter-gunner guiding it down the skids.

*Q.— When down on the bottom and off the skids?*

*A.*—Hook drag rope round axle, and haul gun up on the beach. Then put rammers and sponges on the trail, and fill transporting boxes with ammunition.

### Exercise of Howitzer on Field Carriage.

*Q.—Give the stations and duties in this exercise?*

*A.*—Quarter-gunner, charge of ammunition and spare articles.

No. 1, Captain, rear of breech to the right; is captain of the piece, points and fires, superintends orders, and gives orders in absence of officer.

No. 2, rear of breech to left; closes vent, puts in primer.

No. 3, right side of muzzle; sponges and rams home.

No. 4, left side of muzzle; receives and enters ammunition.

No. 5, rear, and outside of right wheel; assists at right wheel.

No. 6, rear, and outside of left wheel; passes ammunition, and assists at left wheel.

No. 7, five yards rear of right wheel; assists at right wheel, tends bolt of trail wheel, and trail handspike.

No. 8, five yards rear of left wheel; passes ammunition, and assists at left wheel.

No. 9, with No. 7, assists at right wheel.

No. 10, with No. 8, assists at left wheel.

*Q.— What are the words of command?*

*A.*—Preparatory—Man the howitzer!
1. Sponge!
2. Load!
3. Point!
4. Fire!
5. Secure the howitzer!

*Q.—At the preparatory order, what are the duties?*

*A.*—The men go to their stations, as above.

No. 3 takes sponge and rammer.

No. 6 unbolts trail wheel, and ships handspike in socket of trail.

Transporting boxes placed about 25 yards in rear of gun.

Drag rope deposited with ammunition boxes.

*Q.—At the word "sponge?"*

*A.*—No. 3 sponges.

No. 2 serves vent.

Quarter-gunner gets a round from ammunition box, or from one of the men's pouches, and if shell or shrapnel, holds it for officer to adjust fuze.

*Q.*—*At the word "load?"*

*A.*—The charge is passed from quarter-gunner to No. 8—from No. 8 to No. 6—No. 6 to No. 4, who enters it into muzzle.

No. 3 rams home to mark.

No. 2 puts in primer, and covers it with his hand until Nos. 3 and 4 have withdrawn to their stations outside of the wheels.

*Q.*—*At the word "point?"*

*A.*—Officer of gun puts up sight as directed by officer in command.

Captain of gun elevates.

No. 9 trains with the trail handspike.

Captain of gun then goes back to end of laniard, and stands on quarter of breech outside of wheel.

No. 2 stands outside of left wheel; Nos. 3 and 4 fall back, and the rest take the stations first assigned them.

*Q.*—*At the word "fire?"*

*A.*—Captain of gun fires at the word.

No. 2 closes vent.

Nos. 4, 6, 8 go to left wheel; Nos. 5, 7, 9 to right wheel, taking hold of spokes ready to wheel forward, as may be directed by officer in command.

*Q.*—*At the word, " secure the howitzer?"*

*A.*—Quarter-gunner secures the transporting boxes, and gets ready the lashing.

Captain coils lock-laniard around lock.

No. 7 bolts trail wheel.

Nos. 8, 9 hook on and lead out drag rope.

No. 3 may carry sponge and rammer if the firing is only suspended, and so may No. 7 carry the trail handspike.

Then wheel the piece to the ammunition boxes and place on the axles, ready for transportation.

### Embarking the Howitzer.

*Q.—In this exercise, what is the first thing to be done?*

*A.*—Take the transporting boxes off the axles and put them in the boat separately. Then put the pouches into the boat, and lay the skids and secure them.

*Q.— What next?*

*A.*—Bring the field carriage down to the skids, with a wheel resting on each, point the trail towards the boat, and pass in the drag rope.

*Q.—State the operation of getting the gun in?*

*A.*—Nos. 3, 4, 5, 6, 7, 8 divide at the wheels, and take hold of spokes; No. 14 ships trail handspike, and tends it with No. 15; the rest of the men go into the boat and take hold of drag rope.

*Q.—At the word " heave?"*

*A.*—The men at the wheels bear up the carriage on the skids; those in boat haul on drag rope; the two at the trail bear it up so that the quarter-gunner can get hold of trail handspike and guide it fairly.

*Q.— When the gun is in, who pass in the skids?*
*A.*—Nos. 3, 4, 5, 6 unhook and pass them in.

*Q.—How is the howitzer shifted to the boat carriage?*
*A.*—By reversing the orders, Nos. 1, 2 and 3 for shifting to the field carriage.

### Notes.

*Q.—Why should the utmost care be taken in fully providing everything in a boat expedition?*
*A.*—Because after leaving the ship it may be impossible to remedy the deficiency of even a trivial article.

*Q.— What are the chief purposes of boat howitzers?*
*A.*—1. To attack small vessels that are lightly armed, and without protection to their crews.
2. To fight other armed boats.
3. To cover the landing of regular troops.

*Q.—When should the landing of seamen be avoided?.*
*A.*—When opposed by good infantry, or when the object would take the men too far away from their boats, which should be the base of operations.

*Q.—Do the 12-pounders and 24-pounders require tackles to run them out?*

*A.*—The 12-pounders do not—the 24-pounders may.

*Q.—Are breechings necessary?*

*A.*—They are not, as the recoil is fully controlled by the compressors.

*Q.—How do you lessen the recoil of the field carriage on smooth ground?*

*A.*—By taking out the pin of the trail wheel, and turning it up on the trail.

*Q.—When and where may the shrapnel be effectually used?*

*A.*—It may be used effectually when the dispersion of common canister becomes too great, and where uncovered masses of men are in view, it takes the place of the ordinary shell to a great extent, and is designed to burst just in front of troops, scattering its balls among them.

*Q.—How many balls are contained in a 12 and 24-pounder shrapnel?*

*A.*—80 in the 12-pounder, and 175 in the 24-pounder.

*Q.—What is the force of the bursting charge?*

*A.*—Just enough to break the shrapnel open, and allow the balls to fly forwards with the velocity derived from the gun's charge of powder.

*Q.—How are the sights marked?*

A.—Similar terms are used in marking the sight and fuze.

*Q.— Give an example?*

A.—If the fuze is cut to two seconds, and the piece elevated by the sight to the line on it marked two seconds, the shrapnel will burst about 500 yards from the gun.

*Q.—And how far will it then spread its balls?*

A.—At least 150 yards with effect.

*Q.— Then upon what do the conditions for good effect depend?*

A.—Mainly on a correct knowledge of the distance.

*Q.— What do you consider the most effective projectile for the howitzer generally?*

A.—The shrapnel.

*Q.— When may shell be used?*

A.—When the enemy is sheltered, especially in the quarters of small craft or merchantmen, and when material of any kind is to be set on fire.

*Q.—At what distance is canister only required?*

A.—At about 200 yards.

*Q.— What kind of fuze is generally fitted to the shell and shrapnel of the Navy howitzer?*

A.—The Bormann fuze.

*Q.—What has been the effect of the introduction of the 12-pounder rifled howitzer?*

*A.*—It has greatly extended the effective range and accuracy of the boat and field artillery.

*Q.—At what distance have the solid shot and shells of these howitzers effective penetration against ordinary wooden vessels?*

*A.*—At any distance which the elevation allowed by the carriages will reach.

*Q.—At what distance can shrapnel disable men and horses?*

*A.*—2000 yards.

*Q.—What is the objection to firing grape and canister from these rifled guns?*

*A.*—It injures the grooves, and the irregular motion given to the mass diminishes the effect.

*Q.—Suppose, however, they are used?*

*A.*—Then the balls should always be of lead.

*Q.—Why is the ammunition for the boat howitzer "fixed?"*

*A.*—For greater convenience in loading, and to avoid all difficulties.

*Q.—The guns being of bronze, should they be brightened?*

*A.*—By no means; it is prohibited to do so.

## GUNPOWDER.

*Q.— What is gunpowder ?*

*A.*—It is composed of saltpetre, charcoal and sulphur.

*Q.—In what proportions ?*

*A.*—The powder for the Navy is made of 75 parts saltpetre, 15 parts of charcoal, and 10 parts of sulphur.

*Q.— What is the nature of this mixture ?*

*A.*—It is both explosive and propellent.

*Q.—Is it instantaneous in its explosion?*

*A.*—Apparently so; but in reality the whole of the charge of powder in a gun is not burned until the shot has nearly reached the muzzle.

*Q.— What are the essential ingredients to the explosion of gunpowder ?*

*A.*—The saltpetre and charcoal; the sulphur being added to give firmness and consistency to the grains, and prevent them from crumbling.

*Q.—Is it necessary that all the ingredients should be pure ?*

*A.*—Yes; especially the saltpetre.

*Q.— When powder is first made will it not absorb moisture rapidly ?*

*A.*—Yes; and quickly become worthless.

*Q.—Then how is this prevented?*

A.—By pressing, breaking it into grains, and glazing it.

*Q.—Why are the grains made larger for cannon than for muskets?*

A.—Because in small quantities the large grains do not show their strength as much as small grains.

*Q.—What is the reason of this?*

A.—The combustion is slower.

*Q.—What degree of heat is required to explode gunpowder?*

A.—600 degrees.

*Q.—How is gunpowder proved for the Navy?*

A.—By passing the grains through standard sieves—by ascertaining its density—and by trying its initial velocity from the gun pendulum.

*Q.—What is meant by "initial velocity?"*

A.—When applied to a shot it means the velocity with which it leaves the muzzle of the gun. When applied to powder, it indicates the *force* which is required to give a shot, of a certain fixed weight and calibre, such initial velocity when fired with a certain fixed charge.

*Q.—What is the initial velocity required for cannon powder?*

A.—The cannon powder should have strength sufficient to give a 6-pounder ball an initial velocity of not less than 1,500 feet, and not more than 1,550 feet.

*Q.—And for musket powder?*

*A.*—The same.

*Q.—If powder is damaged by being wet, is it then worthless?*

*A.*—By no means; it can be re-worked, the saltpetre being always of value.

*Q.— What is the regulation in reference to damaged powder?*

*A.*—It must be returned to the magazines, for the purpose of saving the saltpetre, and is never to be thrown away by cruising ships, but returned to the United States by the first opportunity.

*Q.— What would be the effect of a charge of fulminating powder in a gun?*

*A.*—It would perhaps burst it, without throwing the ball even a short distance.

*Q.—Is it possible to make powder uniform in in density?*

*A.*—No. And therefore in *measuring* the charges for a gun errors in weight frequently occur.

*Q.— What description of powder has been designed for the XV-in. guns?*

*A.*—Powder with grains nearly the size of a cubic inch.

*Q.—For what reason?*

*A.*—It was supposed that such would give as much or more velocity to the ball without straining the gun as the ordinary cannon powder.

*Q.—Has experiment proved this to be coreect?*

*A.*—No. The velocity is much less, and it is certain that all the grains of the large size are not burned. The regulation now is to use the ordinary cannon powder with these guns.

## HOUSING GUNS.

*Q.—State the duties of No. 1?*

*A.*—No. 1 directs gun to be laid square in the port and run in to taut breeching, and if gun is loaded to draw the load.

*Q.— What are the duties of Nos. 3 and 4?*

*A.*—Place housing trucks before the front trucks.

*Q.— What next?*

*A.*—The gun is run up close against housing chocks, and the chocking quoins placed square up behind rear trucks.

*Q.— What are the duties of Nos. 9 and 10?*

*A.*—Nos. 9 and 10 raise breech to free the bed

and quoin, which are removed by No. 2. Then lower breech upon axletree.

*Q.— Why?*

*A.*—So that if the gun breaks adrift, the muzzle will take the upper port sill.

*Q.— Who lower the port sill, if on lower decks?*

*A.*—The port tacklemen.

*Q.—How is the port then secured?*

*A.*—Nos. 5 and 7 bring port bar to Nos. 3 and 4, who put it across the port, hook port hooks in ring-bolts in port lids, and drive in the keys.

*Q.— What is done by the rest of the men?*

*A.*—Shift side-tackles from training bolts to side-tackle bolts, haul them taut, and expend them between the blocks.

*Q.— What are the further duties of Nos. 3, 4?*

*A.*—To pass frapping lashing round both parts of breeching in front of brackets, and assisted by the nearest men bowse it taut; place gromet over muzzle and housing hook, and lash the two parts together.

*Q.—If the housing bolt is an eye-bolt, what is necessary?*

*A.*—A toggle to keep gromet in place.

*Q.—In bad weather what else is necessary in housing guns?*

*A.*—To hook the train-tackle, bowse it taut, and

expend the ends through the ringbolt and round rear axle.

*Q.—How would you house guns mounted on truck carriages in bad weather on other decks?*

*A.*—In the same way generally, excepting that upper half ports and port bucklers must be put in and secured.

*Q.—When there are no housing chocks provided, what may be used?*

*A.*—The ordinary chocking quoins.

*Q.—What is an additional security?*

*A.*—To take off rear trucks, and tighten muzzle lashing by raising the breech.

## GETTING IN GUNS ON COVERED DECKS.

*Q.—Explain the manner of getting a gun in on covered decks; what is the first operation?*

*A.*—The gun being alongside in the lighter, brace the yard over the port, secure lizard round the yard five or six feet outside of ship, and hook top burtons outside of lizard.

*Q.—What next?*

*A.*—Haul taut and bring equal strain on burtons

and lifts, hook rolling tackle on opposite side of yard, and bowse it taut.

*Q.—How do you secure the gun purchase?*

*A.*—Pass the end of its pendant through thimble of lizard, and make it fast round the topmast just above the lower cap.

*Q.—How do you sling the gun?*

*A.*—Place one bight of the slings under neck of cascabel, and pass the lashing round chase forward of the trunnions far enough to let them drop into the carriage, without bringing too great a pressure of the slings against the upper port sill. Then hook or toggle the gun purchase to the outer bight of slings and bowse away.

*Q.— What other preparations are necessary?*

*A.*—Bore a hole in the deck, as near as possible over the rear end of carriage, and in line with middle of port; pass the upper end of a gurnet through this hole, turn in the thimble and hook the pendant-tackle. Then lay a tackle across the deck ready for bowsing the gun into its carriage through the port.

*Q.— When are these hooked?*

*A.*—When the breech of the gun is above the port sill, hook both of them to cascabel and bowse away.

*Q.— When is the time to lower?*

*A.*—When the slings bear hard against the upper port sill, lower steadily the gun purchase, haul on the gurnet until the breech of gun is high enough to clear capsquare bolts and enter the carriage, then bowse away on the thwartship-tackle till the trunnions are over the holes, lowering the purchase as required to bring the gun into place. To avoid chafe, the ports should be lined with plank.

### Taking in Guns "Over All."

*Q.—How do you get a gun in over all?*

*A.*—If the gun is to be mounted on the spar deck, place the carriage in the gangway, if on the main deck, close to the main hatchway on that deck; sling the gun slightly breech heavy, and in place of the gurnet, hook the stay purchase for lowering the gun into its carriage.

### Getting out Guns through Ports.

*Q.—How is this operation performed?*

*A.*—Secure the yard and sling the gun the same as getting in guns; hook gurnet and haul it taut, hook gun purchase and sway away. As soon as the trunnions are clear of carriage haul it from under the gun, ease away gurnet, and let gun go out of port. When it is perpendicular to the purchase, unhook the gurnet and lower away into lighter.

*Q.—Suppose the gun is to be taken out over all?*

*A.*—Use the stay-tackle in place of the gurnet, hooking it to same end of slings as the gun purchase; and the lashings of the slings are to be passed as near the trunnions as possible.

### Dismounting and Mounting Guns on Covered Decks.

*Q.— What is the Griolet purchase ?*

*A.*—A purchase for dismounting guns on covered decks.

*Q.—Describe it ?*

*A.*—It is composed of a *toggle block* of wood, to be placed in the muzzle of the gun, the outer end, or head, being a little the largest, and having two sheaves in it so as to form the lower block of the *muzzle purchase.*

A double *cascabel block* of iron, to shackle to or fit the jaws of the cascabel, the sheave pins having eyes to hitch the standing part of the purchase to.

Two iron *treble blocks,* one for the *muzzle* and the other for the *breech* purchase.

*Q.—Explain the manner of using this purchase?*

*A.*—Run the gun in, bring the muzzle under the housing bolt, and the breech under the hole bored in the deck to receive the screw bolt of the upper block of *breech purchase.*

*Q.—How should this hole be bored ?*

*A.*—Through the plank in the deck as nearly abreast the middle of port as the beams will allow, giving the block room to play clear of beams and carlines.

*Q.— With a gun's crew of 12 men, how is the*

*operation of dismounting a gun performed—what are the words of command?*

*A.*—1. Stand by to dismount!
2. Run in!
3. Dismount!

*Q.—At the word, "Stand by to dismount?"*

*A.*—The quarter-gunner of the division on the deck above removes screw tap, and stands ready to place the washer, key and unkey the bolt of breech purchase. All the gun numbers except 1, 2, 3 and 4 man the train-tackle.

*Q.—At the word "Run In?"*

*A.*—Nos. 1, 2 remove breeching from cascabel, Nos. 7 and 8 from side-shackle; Nos. 1 and 2 then throw its bight over reinforce, and No. 1 removes sight bar.

*Q.—When the gun is in position?*

*A.*—Nos. 1 and 2 fix upper and lower block of breech purchase, and secure it to cascabel; Nos. 3, 4 chock fore trucks, provide muzzle purchase, and assisted by Nos. 5, 6, adjust its upper block; Nos. 5, 6 unshackle breeching from ship's side, shove toggle block into bore and back it to breech purchase.

Nos. 7, 8 unkey and throw back capsquares and choke or hitch luffs of side-tackles.

Nos. 9 and 10 provide the breech purchase, and assist Nos. 1 and 2 in adjusting it.

No. 11 chokes or hitches luff of train-tackle, provides and hooks tackle of *muzzle* purchase, belays and lowers.

No. 12 provides and hooks tackle of *breech* purchase, belays and lowers.

*Q.—After these preparations are all made, how do the gun numbers divide themselves ?*

*A.*—To bowse upon both purchase falls together, or they man the breech-tackle alone, according to the position of the gun in battery.

*Q.—At the word " Dismount ?"*

*A.*—Sway the gun out of the carriage; then Nos. 3 and 4 attend chocking quoins, while No. 11 tends train-tackle if required.

*Q.— What are then the duties of the other numbers ?*

*A.*—All, except Nos. 11 and 12, who attend purchase falls, unhook the side-tackle falls, and remove the old carriage.

*Q.—At the word " Mount ?"*

*A.*—They bring the new carriage into position ready for mounting.

*Q.—At the word " Lower ?"*

*A.*—Nos. 11 and 12 lower the gun into its place, and the rest proceed to reverse what they had done in dismounting.

*Q.— Can guns be dismounted on covered decks by any other means than this Griolet purchase ?*

*A.*—Yes. By means of a muzzle lashing, the runner, and the train-tackles, assisted by the handspikes.

*Q.—Explain the operation?*

*A.*—Run in, lay the gun square under the housing-bolt, remove bed and quoin, elevate and secure muzzle as in the housing position. Then unkey and throw back capsquare, bowse the breech of gun up clear of the carriage by the train-tackle hooked into the eye of a runner, the block of which hooks into an eye-bolt in the beam over the gun.

### Throwing Guns Overboard.

*Q.—In a gale of wind, how is a gun thrown overboard?*

*A.*—Take out the cascabel chock, and place a selvagee strap in the jaws; hook the double block of train-tackle into the housing bolt over the port, and the single block into the selvagee strap; remove the capsquares, and put a round block of wood on sill of port high enough to let the chase rest on it when slightly depressed; then raise the breech as much as possible without lifting the gun out of the carriage. When all is ready, watch the roll, give the word, "all together, launch," and bowse the gun out of the port by the train-tackle.

*Q.—How can the operation be assisted?*

*A.*—By the handspikes, placed on each side under the breech; and if there is no rolling motion, additional handspikes should be placed under the carriage also to assist in launching.

*Q.*—*In throwing guns overboard to lighten a ship aground, what is to be attended to?*

*A.*—To have a buoy to each gun, the rope of sufficient length, and strong enough to weigh the gun.

*Q.*—*What is the best way to attach the buoy rope?*

*A.*—Clinch it, or splice an eye in the end which goes over the cascabel, take a half hitch with the bight over the chase, and stop it with spun yarn.

## GENERAL QUESTIONS IN GUNNERY.

*Q.*—*What are the essential qualities in a good gun?*

*A.*—Accuracy, range, and penetration.

*Q.*—*What are the relative values of these three qualities?*

*A.*—Accuracy is *always* essential; and range combined with accuracy is also of the first importance. Without accuracy range is of little value. Penetration, as an expression of *force*, is also of great importance, but depends very much on the character of the projectile used.

*Q.—On what do these three qualities depend?*

*A.*—In spherical *solid* shot directly upon the charge of the gun and calibre of the shot.

*Q.—And why? How does range so depend, for instance?*

*A.*—Because upon the charge depends the initial velocity; and upon the *mass* of the shot depends the power to maintain that velocity by overcoming the resistance of the air; and the mass is always in proportion to the cube of the diameter or calibre.

*Q.—How does accuracy depend on them?*

*A.*—Supposing the gun to be properly aimed, accuracy depends on the power to reach the object fired at; in other words, on the velocity and the power of preserving it.

*Q.—How does penetration depend on them?*

*A.*—Penetration depends on the *momentum* of the shot, and this momentum is a compound of the weight (or mass) and velocity.

*Q.—Is it the same with shells as with solid shot?*

*A.*—Not exactly. A shell having less weight than a solid shot of the same calibre, has less power of overcoming resistance, and much therefore depends on the internal character of the shell.

*Q.—How is it with rifled projectiles?*

*A.*—These depend on many other causes for success, besides the charge and calibre—such as the mode of rifling, shape and character of projectiles, the proportion of its length to its weight, etc.

*Q.— What are the principal causes which affect the accuracy of spherical projectiles, or in other words, make them deviate from their proper or normal path?*

*A.*—Those which act on the projectile while it is in the bore of the piece, and those which act upon it after it has left the bore.

*Q.— What does the first class of causes include?*

*A.*—All that affects the initial velocity, and gives rotation to the ball.

*Q.— What does the second include?*

*A.*—The action of the air.

*Q.— What are the principal causes that affect the initial velocity?*

*A.*—Variations in weights of powder and ball, the manner of loading, the temperature of the piece, and the balloting of the ball along the bore.

*Q.— What is the principal cause of deviation?*

*A.*—The rotation of the ball combined with the resistance of the air.

*Q.—Suppose the ball is truly spherical and homogeneous—that is, the centre of gravity is in the centre of its figure, how is rotation produced?*

*A.*—By the balloting or bounding of the ball along the bore, owing to the windage.

*Q.—On what does the direction of rotation depend?*

*A.*—On the side of the projectile which strikes the surface of the bore last—if it strike on the upper side, the front surface of the ball will move upward; if on the lower side, this surface will move downward.

*Q.—On what does the velocity of rotation from this cause depend?*

*A.*—On the windage, or depth of the indentations in the bore, the charge being the same.

*Q.—Suppose the centre of gravity does not coincide with the centre of figure, how does the rotation take place?*

*A.*—It generally takes place around the centre of gravity; and the deviation is said to be produced by *eccentricity.*

*Q.—State the action of this cause in general terms?*

*A.*—The front surface of the ball moves toward the side of the bore on which the centre of gravity is situated; and knowing the position of this centre of gravity, it is easy to foretell the direction in which the ball will rotate.

*Q.—In the case of an eccentric ball, when is the velocity of rotation greatest?*

*A.*—When the line joining the centre of gravity and figure is perpendicular to the axis of the bore.

*Q.—How is the* range *affected by rotation in a* spherical and concentric *ball?*

*A.*—It is shortened or lengthened, as the motion of the front surface is downward or upward.

*Q.—How is the range affected by rotation in a* spherical and eccentric *ball?*

*A.*—By the position of the centre of gravity (or the heavier hemisphere,) in the bore. If placed upwards the range is increased, downwards it is decreased.

*Q.—Can you give an example from experimental practice of the results of placing the centre of gravity in different positions in the bore?*

*A.*—Yes; the following results were obtained by the experiments of Rear Admiral Dahlgren:

Placed 90 degrees up, the range was 1,415 yards.
Placed 90 degrees down, the range was 1,264 y'ds.
Placed inwards, the range was 1,329 yards.
Placed 45 degrees *up and in*, the range was 1,360 yards.

*Q.—With Navy shells, how is the position of the centre of gravity uniformly fixed and determined?*

*A.*—Formerly it was the habit to strap them to the sabots with the fuze at an angle of 45 degrees, and in loading, the fuze was always to be placed upwards in the bore. This sometimes the loader failed to do—and to fix the centre beyond all mistake the shells are now strapped with the fuze *out* and in the axis of the bore.

*Q.—Does the position of the centre of gravity affect the ricochet?*

*A.*—Yes. The number of grazes are increased or diminished, by placing it up or down in the bore.

*Q.—How are projectiles affected by the wind?*

*A.*—The deviating effect of the wind depends on its force, and its direction with regard to the plane of fire.

*Q.—What projectiles are less affected in their flight by this cause?*

*A.*—Large and heavy projectiles, moving with high velocities.

*Q.—Why are the chances of inaccuracy in firing at long ranges much greater than when firing at short ones?*

*A.*—The greater the elevation, the more curved will be the path of the shot, and the effect of any error in pointing is increased by the distance; while the balloting of the shot in the bore and the position of the centre of gravity of the shot will have more time to act in causing deviation, as will also the wind, or partial currents of air.

*Q.—What is meant by the term initial velocity?*

*A.*—The velocity with which a shot leaves the gun.

*Q.—With a charge of one-third the weight of the shot, what is this supposed to be?*

*A.*—About 1,600 feet in a second.

*Q.—Does a wad, or ramming home the charge, affect the initial velocity?*

*A.*—No. The velocity is the same whether the charge is rammed, or a wad used or not.

*Q.—Then what is the use of the wad?*

*A.*—To prevent the shot from shifting in the bore of the gun.

*Q.—Is the initial velocity always the same from the same gun?*

*A.*—No. It depends upon the kind and weight of powder and projectile, the elevation and temperature of the piece when fired.

*Q.—What is meant by the term "remaining velocity?"*

*A.*—The rate with which a ball moves at any given point in its flight, after it has been subjected to the resistance of the air.

*Q.—What is "striking velocity?"*

*A.*—That with which a ball strikes the object.

*Q.—What is the flight of a shot through the air called?*

*A.*—Its trajectory, or the path of the shot.

*Q.—If a gun placed several feet above a horizontal plane is fired at an object distant 1000 yards, and at the same height above the plane, how will the ball move if not acted upon by any other force?*

*A.*—It will continue to move in the direction of

that object through equal spaces in equal times—forever.

*Q.— What other force is it then that acts upon the ball immediately on its leaving the gun, and prevents this movement ?*

*A.*—The force of gravity, which is always constant, and draws the ball to the earth with an accelerated velocity.

*Q.—In the case of a ball fired from a gun several feet above the plane, at an object 1000 yards distant, how soon will it reach the plane ?*

*A.*—In precisely the same time as it would if let fall perpendicularly from the muzzle to the plane.

*Q.—In defining "remaining velocity," you mention the resistance of the air—suppose this force is removed and does not act against the ball, what is the result ?*

*A.*—In that case, large and small, heavy and light balls, when fired with equal velocities and elevations, would have equal ranges.

*Q.—If fired with different velocities ?*

*A.*—Then the ranges would be directly as the velocities.

*Q.—But as the resistance of the air is always active in retarding the ball, upon what description of balls does it thus act with most effect, and under what conditions ?*

*A.*—It acts with greater effect in retarding small

balls than large ones. With greater effect upon balls of little density than upon those of great density. And with greater *proportional* effect upon balls moving with high velocity than upon balls moving with low velocity.

*Q.— What is the measure of the air's resistance?*

*A.*—The difference of pressure before and behind the ball.

*Q.—Explain how the air retards small balls more effectively than large ones?*

*A.*—The absolute resistances they both meet are, (velocities being equal,) as the extent of their surfaces, which are as the squares of their diameters. But their power to overcome resistance are as their weights, which are as the *cubes* of the diameters.

*Q.— Give an example?*

*A.*—Take two balls, one of 3 inches and one of 6 inches diameter. The resistance then is as 9 to 36, or 1 to 4—while the power to overcome it is as 27 to 216, or 1 to 8.

*Q.—How are dense balls less retarded by the air than light balls of equal diameter?*

*A.*—Because although surfaces being equal resistances are equal, yet the power to overcome this resistance being as the weights the denser ball is less retarded.

*Q.—How are balls moving with low velocity re-*

tarded by the air less than those moving with high velocity?

*A.*—When a ball moves with high velocity the air is condensed in front of it, and rarefied behind it; hence it is constantly pressed back by an increased force which is not balanced from behind. When moving with low velocity, this is not the case, the pressure of the air in front and behind is nearly equal, and the ball meets with less resistance.

*Q.*— *What is the* momentum *of a ball?*

*A.*—Its weight multiplied by its velocity when fired.

*Q.*— *What is the direct result upon the gun of this momentum given to the shot?*

*A.*—All the momentum the shot has in one direction, the gun takes in an opposite direction.

*Q.*— *What is this termed?*

*A.*—The *recoil of the gun.*

*Q.*—*How is the* velocity *of this recoil determined?*

*A.*—Divide the momentum of recoil by the weight of gun, and the quotient is the velocity of recoil.

*Q.*—*If both leave the gun at the same rate, which will have the greatest penetration, a large ball or a small one?*

*A.*—The large one, the penetration being in proportion to the diameters.

*Q.*— *With shot of equal diameters?*

*A.*—Then the penetrations are in proportion to the charges.

*Q.—In the event of a gun being likely to fall into the hands of an enemy, how may it be rendered unserviceable?*

*A.*—By driving a nail or rat-tail file into the vent and breaking it off. By firing a shot against the trunnions and breaking them. And brass guns are rendered unserviceable by firing a shot against the chase, which indents them and prevents loading.

*Q.—How can you ascertain the distance of an object by means of the tangent sight of a gun, the height of the object being known?*

*A.*—Point by line of metal to the top of the object; then raise the tangent scale till the top of it and the notch on the muzzle are in line with the foot of the object, and note the length of tangent sight required. Then, by similar triangles, as the length of tangent sight thus required, is to the length of the gun so is the height of the object to the distance required. This, however, can only be done from a fixed battery on shore.

*Q.—In pointing guns by the tangent sights, is the trajectory of the ball affected by the height of the gun above the plane?*

*A.*—No. The trajectory is the same whether the gun is fired from the top of a hill, or from the valley below. The use of the tangent sight in aiming has no effect on the trajectory.

## RANGE TABLES, NOS. 1 AND 2.

These diagrams are intended to show the curves of projectiles fired from different guns with certain charges of powder, and from which the range for any given elevation, or the elevation required for any known distance, is readily determined.

The degrees of elevation are given on the side; and the figures at the head of the diagrams, on the line marked *water line*, represent hundreds of yards. Then to obtain the elevation for any given range, find the range in yards at top of diagram on this *water line*—follow the corresponding vertical line to its intersection with the curved line representing the flight of the projectile from the gun in use, and, opposite the point of intersection, will be found the required elevation on the side of the diagram.

And to get the range for any given elevation, this operation is reversed.

The "sound scale" gives the distance in yards for seconds of time observed between the flash and report of an enemy's gun; and can be used to determine the range of bursting shells.

These diagrams are given as examples—the scale being too small for practical purposes. The intelligent officer, however, will readily construct for his own use other diagrams from the tables of ranges in the ordnance instructions, adapted to particular guns, upon a scale of any size.

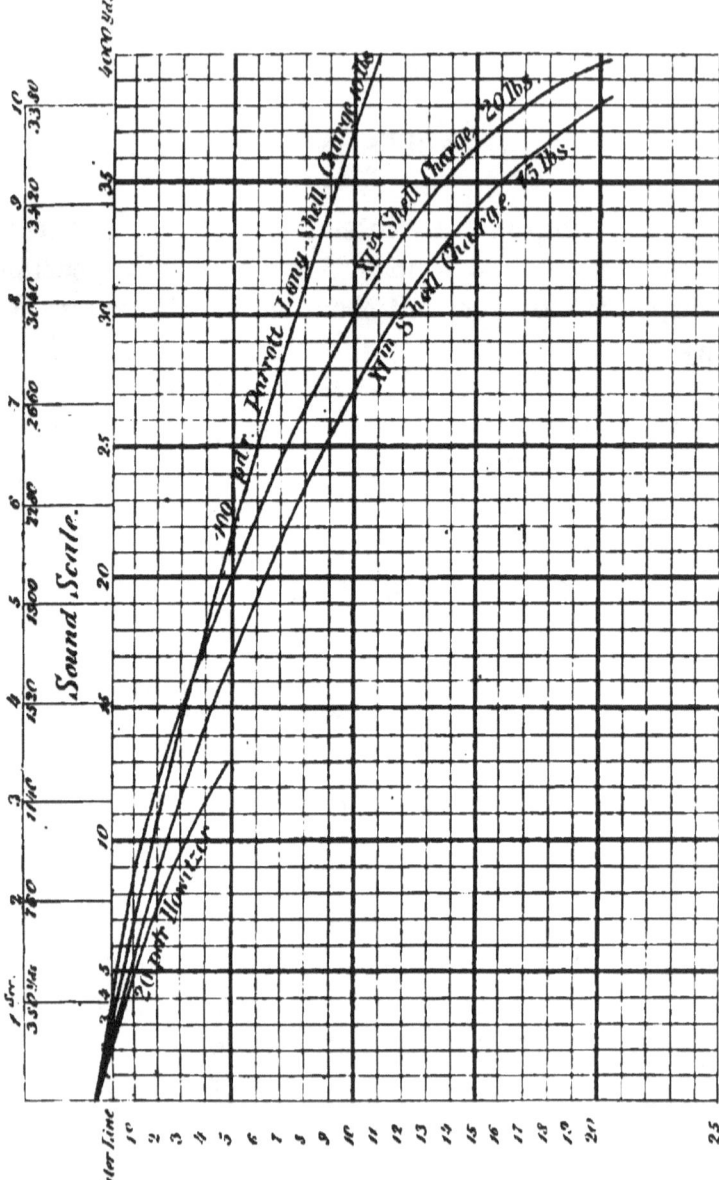

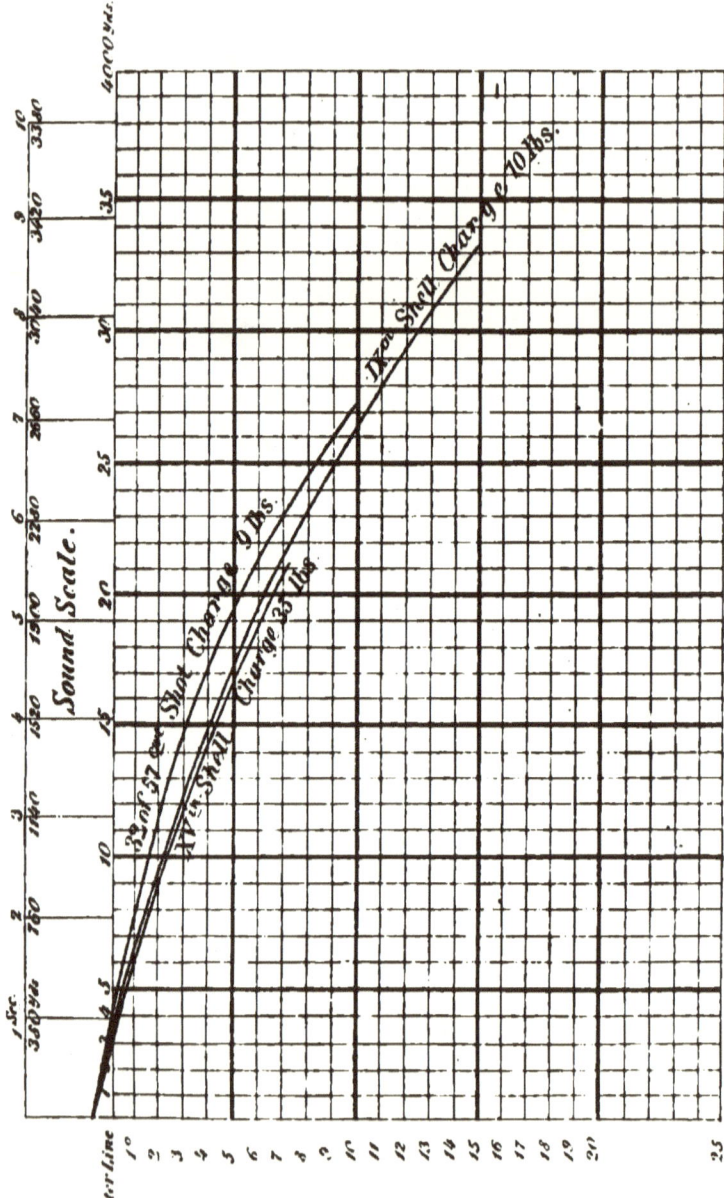

# GRADUATION OF SIGHTS AND MEAN RANGES
## OF
## UNITED STATES NAVAL GUNS.

*(From Results of Practice, by Admiral* DAHLGREN, *United States Navy.)*

## I.

The graduation commences from the bottom of the head of the bar resting on the sight-box.

The aim is supposed to be taken at the water-line of a ship.

| | | 32-POUNDER OF 27 CWT. | | 32-POUNDER OF 33 CWT. | |
|---|---|---|---|---|---|
| Charge.............. | | 4 lbs. | | 4¼ lbs. | |
| Axis of bore above load line....... | | 7 feet. | | 7¼ feet. | |
| Distance between sights.......... | | Old model. 29¼ inches. | New model. 26¼ inches. | 31 inches. | |
| Elevation. | Range. | Graduation. | Graduation. | Range. | Graduation. |
| Degrees. | Yards. | Inches. | Inches. | Yards. | Inches. |
| Level. | 250 | 0.353 | 0.324 | 287 | 0.350 |
| 1° | 545 | 0.746 | 0.684 | 581 | 0.792 |
| 2° | 800 | 1.266 | 1.161 | 857 | 1.343 |
| 3° | 1,047 | 1.801 | 1.652 | 1,140 | 1.909 |
| 4° | 1,278 | 2.337 | 2.144 | 1,398 | 2.478 |
| 5° | 1,469 | 2.870 | 2.633 | 1,598 | 3.044 |
| 6° | 1,637 | 3.398 | 3.116 | ........ | ........ |

## II.

| | 32-POUNDER OF 42 CWT. | | 32-POUNDER OF 57 CWT. | |
|---|---|---|---|---|
| Charge............ | 6 lbs. | | 9 lbs. | |
| Axis of bore above load line....... | 7¼ feet. | | 8 feet. | |
| Distance between sights.......... | Old model. 40.5 inches. | New model. 37.1 inches. | 42.5 inches. | |
| Elevation. | Range. | Graduation. | Graduation. | |
| | | | | |
| Elevation. | Range. | Graduation. | Graduation. | Range. | Graduation. |
| Degrees. | Yards. | Inches. | Inches. | Yards. | Inches. |
| Level. | 318 | 0.446 | 0.408 | 360 | 0.412 |
| 1° | 672 | 1.016 | 0.981 | 760 | 1.042 |
| 2° | 988 | 1.742 | 1.596 | 1,150 | 1.808 |
| 3° | 1,274 | 2.488 | 2.280 | 1,440 | 2.597 |
| 4° | 1,505 | 3.235 | 2.964 | 1,710 | 3.384 |
| 5° | 1,756 | 3.974 | 3.641 | 1,980 | 4.162 |
| 6° | ...... | ...... | ...... | 2,140 | 4.930 |

## III.

| | 8-INCH OF 55 CWT. | | 8-INCH OF 63 CWT. | | |
|---|---|---|---|---|---|
| Charge............... | 7 lbs. | | 9 lbs. | | |
| Shell................. | 51¼ lbs. | | 51¼ lbs. | | |
| Axis of bore above load line................ | 7¼ feet. | | 8 feet. | | |
| Distance betw'n sights. | 37 inches. | | Old model. 43.50 inches. | New model. 38.20 inches. | |
| Elevation. | Range. | Graduation. | Range. | Graduation. | Graduation. |
| Degrees. | Yards. | Inches. | Yards. | Inches. | Inches. |
| Level. | 283 | 0.429 | 330 | 0.460 | 0.402 |
| 1° | 579 | 0.949 | 660 | 1.100 | 0.964 |
| 2° | 869 | 1.603 | 970 | 1.878 | 1.647 |
| 3° | 1,148 | 2.280 | 1,266 | 2.679 | 2.350 |
| 4° | 1,413 | 2.958 | 1,540 | 3.478 | 3.051 |
| 5° | 1,657 | 3.632 | 1,770 | 4.278 | 3.749 |
| 6° | 1,866 | 4.800 | ...... | ...... | ...... |

# RANGES OF GUNS—GRADUATION OF SIGHTS.

## IV.

| | IX-INCH SHELL GUN. | | XI-INCH SHELL GUN. | | XI-INCH SHELL GUN. | |
|---|---|---|---|---|---|---|
| Charge........ | 10 lbs. | | 15 lbs. | | 15 lbs. | |
| Shell......... | 72 lbs. | | 135 lbs. | | 135 lbs. | |
| Axis of bore above load line....... | 10 feet. | | 10 feet. [Screw sloops.] | | 20 feet. [2d deck above water.] | |
| Distance between sights | 39 inches. | | 48 inches. | | 48 inches. | |
| Elevation. | Range. | Graduation. | Range. | Graduation. | Range. | Graduation. |
| Degrees. | Yards. | Inches. | Yards. | Inches. | Yards. | Inches. |
| Level. | 340 | 0.461 | 306 | 0.600 | 420 | 0.87 |
| ............ | 700 | 0.983 | 500 | 0.945 | 700 | 1.48 |
| ............ | 900 | 1.514 | 700 | 1.442 | 900 | 2.01 |
| ............ | 1,100 | 2.073 | 900 | 2.040 | 1,100 | 2.62 |
| ............ | 1,300 | 2.646 | 1,100 | 2.651 | 1,300 | 3.25 |
| ............ | 1,500 | 3.222 | 1,300 | 3.295 | 1,500 | 4.92 |
| ............ | 1,700 | 3.813 | 1,500 | 3.953 | ........ | ........ |
| ............ | ........ | ........ | 1,700 | 4.681 | ........ | ........ |

## V.—APPROXIMATE RANGES

| Class of gun. | Kind of projectile. | Weight of projectile. | Charge, lbs. | Height above plane. | P. B. or 0° | 1° | 2° | 3° | 4° |
|---|---|---|---|---|---|---|---|---|---|
| XV-inch.. | Cored shot | 400 | .... | .... | .... | .... | .... | .... | .... |
|  | Shell | 350 | 35 | .... | 300 | 620 | 920 1.9 | 1,200 3.7 | 1,470 4.3 |
| XI-inch.. | Shell | 136 | 15 | 10 | 306 .84 | 631 1.72 | 918 2.8 | 1,208 3.88 | 1,472 4.9 |
|  | Shell | 136 | 15 | 20 | 421 1.16 | 679 1.96 | 992 3 | 1,257 3.94 | 1,524 4.99 |
|  | Shell | 136 | 20 | 10 | 350 | 700 | 1,000 | 1,340 | 1,660 |
| X-inch... | Shrapnel.. | 141 | 15 | 10 | 295 .8 | 620 1.7 | 910 2.7 | 1,200 3.7 | 1,465 4.7 |
|  | Shell | 103 | 12½ | 11 | 340 | 705 2 | 970 2.9 | 1,230 3.9 | 1,490 4.9 |
|  | Shrapnel.. | 101 | .... | .... | .... | .... | .... | .... | .... |
| IX-inch.. | Shell | 72½ | 10 | 10 | 340 .9 | 700 1.96 | 960 3 | 1,230 4 | 1,465 5.1 |
|  | Shell | .... | 13 | 10 | 350 | 710 | 930 | 1,275 | 1,520 |
|  | Shrapnel. | 75 | 10 | .... | 332 .8 | 718 1.9 | 960 2.9 | 1,215 4 | 1,470 5 |
| VIII-in., 63-cwt... | Shell | 51¼ | 9 | 8 | 330 | 660 1.89 | 970 3.07 | 1,260 4.34 | 1,540 5.32 |
|  | Shrapnel.. | 52 | .... | .... | 340 .9 | 670 1.8 | 930 3 | 1,270 4.2 | 1,550 5.2 |
| VIII-in., 55-cwt... | Shell | 51¼ | 7 | 7½ | 288 | 579 1.7 | 869 2.9 | 1,148 | 1,413 |
|  | Shrapnel.. | 52 | .... | .... | 290 .8 | 590 1.6 | 880 2.8 | 1,160 3.9 | 1,420 4.9 |

## OF SHELL GUNS.

—RANGES IN YARDS.—TIME OF FLIGHT IN SECONDS.

| 5° | 6° | 7° | 8° | 9° | 10° | 11° | 12° | 13° | 14° | 15° |
|---|---|---|---|---|---|---|---|---|---|---|
| ..... | 1,900 | 2,100 | ...... | .... | .... | .... | .... | .... | .... | .... |
| 1,700 | 6.5 | 7.7 | | | | | | | | |
| 5.7 | | | | | | | | | | |
| 1,712 | 1,914 | 2,105 | 2,300 | 2,500 | 2,687 | 2,870 | 3,023 | 3,160 | 3,300 | 3,440 |
| 5.81 | 6.74 | | | | 10.2 | 11.70 | 12.15 | | | |
| 1,757 | 1,950 | 2,140 | ...... | .... | .... | .... | .... | .... | .... | .... |
| 6.04 | | | | | | | | | | |
| 1,975 | 2,255 | 2,490 | 2,690 | 2,870 | 3,025 | 3,175 | 3,305 | 3,435 | 3,550 | 3,650 |
| | | 8.6 | | 10.2 | | 11.8 | | 14 | | 16.5 |
| 1,710 | ...... | ...... | ...... | .... | .... | .... | .... | .... | .... | .... |
| 5.6 | | | | | | | | | | |
| 1,740 | 1,960 | 2,210 | 2,430 | 2,640 | 2,840 | 3,000 | .... | .... | .... | .... |
| 5.8 | 6.7 | | 8.5 | | 10.1 | | | | | |
| 1,700 | 1,920 | 2,120 | 2,305 | 2,475 | 2,630 | 2,780 | 2,920 | 3,190 | 3,245 | 3,300 |
| 5.96 | | 8 | | 8.6 | 11.3 | 12.9 | | 13.5 | | 14.7 |
| 1,750 | 1,980 | 2,200 | 2,395 | 2,580 | 2,750 | 2,910 | 3,055 | 3,190 | 3,320 | 3,450 |
| 1,690 | ...... | ...... | ...... | .... | .... | .... | .... | .... | .... | .... |
| 5.9 | | | | | | | | | | |
| 1,770 | ...... | ...... | ...... | .... | .... | .... | .... | .... | .... | .... |
| 6.32 | | | | | | | | | | |
| 1.775 | ...... | ...... | ...... | .... | .... | .... | .... | .... | .... | .... |
| 6.2 | | | | | | | | | | |
| 1,657 | 1,866 | ...... | 2,315 | .... | 2,600 | .... | .... | .... | .... | .... |
| 1,660 | ...... | ...... | ...... | .... | .... | .... | .... | .... | .... | .... |
| 5.8 | | | | | | | | | | |

## VI.—APPROXIMATE RANGES OF

| Class of gun. | Kind of projectile.* | W'ht of projectile. | Charge. | Height above plane. | P. B. or 0° | 1° | 2° | 3° | 4° |
|---|---|---|---|---|---|---|---|---|---|
| 32-pounder of 57 cwt. | Shot...... | 32 | 9 | 8 | 360 | 760<br>2.2 | 1,150<br>3.4 | 1,440<br>4.3 | 1,710<br>5.3 |
|  | Shell..... | 26 | 6 | .... | .... | 800<br>2.2 | 1,100<br>3.3 | 1,350<br>4.2 | 1,570<br>5 |
|  | Shrapnel... | 32 | .... | .... | 360 | 760<br>2.2 | 1,150<br>3.4 | 1,440<br>4.3 | 1,710<br>5.3 |
| 32-pounder of 42 cwt. | Shot....... | 32 | 6 | 8¼ | 318 | 672 | 983 | 1,274 | 1,505 |
|  | Shell...... | 26 | 6 | .... | 330<br>.7 | 700<br>1.8 | 1,020<br>2.9 | 1,300<br>4.2 | 1,500<br>5.1 |
|  | Shrapnel... | 32 | .... | .... | 318<br>.8 | 672<br>1.8 | 983<br>2.9 | 1,274<br>3.8 | 1,505<br>4.8 |
| 32-pounder of 33 cwt. | Shot....... | 32 | 4¼ | 7¼ | 287 | 581 | 857 | 1,140 | 1,398 |
|  | Shot....... | 32 | 4¼ | 15¼ | 366<br>1.1 | 655<br>2 | 929<br>2.9 | 1,152<br>3.9 | 1,385<br>4.9 |
|  | Shell...... | 26 | 4¼ | 7¼ | 298 | 661 | 952 | 1,218 | 1,416 |
|  | Shrapnel... | 32 | 4¼ | 7¼ | 297<br>1 | 581<br>1.8 | 857<br>2.7 | 1,140<br>3.8 | 1,398<br>4.9 |
| 32-pounder of 27 cwt. | Shot...... | 32 | 4 | 7 | 250<br>.7 | 545<br>1.4 | 800<br>2.6 | 1,047<br>3.7 | 1,278<br>4.5 |
|  | Shell...... | 26 | .... | .... | .... | .... | .... | .... | .... |
|  | Shrapnel.. | 32 | .... | .... | 250<br>.7 | 545<br>1.4 | 800<br>2.6 | 1.047<br>3.7 | 1,278<br>4.5 |
| 24-pounder howitzer. | Shell...... | 20 | 2 | .... | .... | 541<br>2. | 760<br>2.9 | 960<br>3.8 | 1,140<br>4.8 |
|  | Shrapnel.. | 26 | .... | .... | .... | 540<br>1.8 | 760<br>2.9 | 960<br>4. | 1,140<br>5. |
| 12-pdr. heavy howitzer. | Shell...... | 10 | 1 | .... | .... | 516<br>1.9 | 715<br>2.8 | 875<br>3.6 | 995<br>4.3 |
|  | Shrapnel.. | 13 | .... | .... | .... | 498<br>1.8 | 630<br>2.6 | 845<br>3.7 | 1,000<br>4.4 |
| 12-pdr. light howitzer. | Shell...... | 9 | .... | .... | .... | .... | .... | .... | .... |
|  | Shrapnel.. | 12 | 625 | .... | .... | .... | .... | .... | .... |

## SHOT GUNS AND HOWITZERS.

— RANGES IN YARDS. — TIME OF FLIGHT IN SECONDS.

| 5° | 6° | 7° | 8° | 9° | 10° | 11° | 12° | 13° | 14° | 15° |
|---|---|---|---|---|---|---|---|---|---|---|
| 1,930<br>6.6 | 2,140<br>7.7 | 2,310 | 2,460 | 2,610 | 2,731<br>10.7 | .... | .... | .... | .... | .... |
| 1,760<br>6 | .... | .... | .... | .... | .... | .... | .... | .... | .... | .... |
| 1,930<br>6.6 | .... | .... | .... | .... | .... | .... | .... | .... | .... | .... |
| 1,756 | .... | .... | .... | .... | .... | .... | .... | .... | .... | .... |
| 1,750<br>6.2 | .... | .... | .... | .... | .... | .... | .... | .... | .... | .... |
| 1,756<br>5.8 | .... | .... | .... | .... | .... | .... | .... | .... | .... | .... |
| 1,598 | .... | .... | .... | .... | .... | .... | .... | .... | .... | .... |
| .... | .... | .... | .... | .... | .... | .... | .... | .... | .... | .... |
| 1,649 | .... | .... | .... | .... | .... | .... | .... | .... | .... | .... |
| 1,598<br>6 | .... | .... | .... | .... | .... | .... | .... | .... | .... | .... |
| 1,469<br>5.4 | 1,637<br>6.3 | .... | .... | .... | .... | .... | .... | .... | .... | .... |
| 1,469<br>5.4 | 1,637<br>6.3 | .... | .... | .... | .... | .... | .... | .... | .... | .... |
| .... | .... | .... | .... | .... | .... | .... | .... | .... | .... | .... |
| .... | .... | .... | .... | .... | .... | .... | .... | .... | .... | .... |
| 1,085<br>5 | .... | .... | .... | .... | .... | .... | .... | .... | .... | .... |
| 1,150<br>5.2 | .... | .... | .... | .... | .... | .... | .... | .... | .... | .... |
| .... | .... | .... | .... | .... | .... | .... | .... | .... | .... | .... |
| .... | .... | .... | .... | .... | .... | .... | .... | .... | .... | .... |

## VII.—APPROXIMATE RANGES

| Class of gun. | Kind of projectile. | Weight of Projectile. | Charge, lbs. | Height above plane. | P, B, or 0°. | 1° | 2° | 3° |
|---|---|---|---|---|---|---|---|---|
| Parrot — 8-inch, or 150 pdr. | Solid shot... | .... | .... | .... | .... | .... | .... | .... |
| | Hollow shot. | .... | .... | .... | .... | .... | .... | .... |
| | Long shell.. | 155 | 16 | .... | .... | .... | .... | .... |
| | Short shell.. | .... | .... | .... | .... | .... | .... | .... |
| Parrot—100 pdr. | Solid shot... | 99¼ | No. 7 10 | .... | .... | .... | .... | .... |
| | Hollow shot. | 80 | 10 | .... | .... | .... | .... | .... |
| | Long shell.. | 100 | 10 | .... | .... | .... | .... | 1,400 4¼ |
| | Short shell.. | 80 | 10 | .... | .... | .... | .... | .... |
| Parrot—60 pdr.. | Shrapnel.... | .... | .... | .... | .... | .... | .... | .... |
| | Shot........ | .... | .... | .... | .... | .... | .... | .... |
| | Shell ...... | .... | .... | .... | .... | .... | .... | .... |
| | Shrapnel.... | .... | .... | .... | .... | .... | .... | .... |
| Parrot—30 pdr.. | Shot........ | .... | .... | .... | .... | .... | .... | .... |
| | Shell ...... | 29 | Can. 8¼ | .... | .... | .... | .... | .... |
| | Shrapnel.... | .... | .... | .... | .... | .... | .... | .... |
| Parrot—20 pdr.. | Shot........ | .... | .... | .... | .... | .... | .... | .... |
| | Shell........ | 18¾ | Can. 2 | .... | .... | .... | .... | .... |
| | Shrapnel.... | 19¼ | Can. 2 | .... | .... | 620 1¼ | 950 3¼ | .... |
| Dahlgren—20 pdr.......... | Shot........ | .... | Can. 2 | .... | .... | .... | .... | .... |
| | Shell ....... | 20 | 2 | .... | .... | .... | .... | 1,280 |
| | Shrapnel.... | .... | 2 | .... | .... | .... | .... | .... |
| Dahlgren—12 pdr. ........ | Shot........ | .... | Can. 1 | .... | .... | .... | .... | .... |
| | Shell........ | 12 | 1 | .... | .... | .... | .... | .... |
| | Shrapnel.... | .... | 1 | .... | .... | .... | .... | .... |

# OF RIFLE GUNS.

DEGREES—RANGES IN YARDS—TIME OF FLIGHT IN SECONDS.

| 3¼° | 3¾° | 4° | 5° | 10° | 15° | 20° | 25° | 30° | 35° |
|---|---|---|---|---|---|---|---|---|---|
| | | | | | | | | | |
| | | | | | | | | | |
| | | | 2,100<br>6½ | | | | | | |
| | | | | | | | | | |
| | | | 2,200<br>6¼ | 3,810<br>13 | 5,030<br>18¼ | 6,125<br>22¼ | 6,910<br>29 | | |
| | | | | | 5,190<br>19 | 6,383<br>23 | 7,180<br>29¼ | 7,988<br>32¼ | 8,453<br>36¾ |
| 1,450<br>4¼ | | 1,700<br>5¼ | 2,150<br>6¼ | 3,700<br>13 | 4,790<br>18 | 5,853<br>21¼ | 6,820<br>28 | | |
| | | | | | | | | 7,810<br>32¼ | |
| | | | | | | | | | |
| | | | | | | | | | |
| | | | | | | | | | |
| | | | | | | | | | |
| 1,500<br>4¼ | | | 2,200<br>6⅞ | 3,500<br>12¼ | 4,800<br>17⅜ | 5,700<br>21¼ | 6,700<br>27 | | |
| | | | | | | | | | |
| | 1,500<br>4¼ | | 2,100<br>6¼ | 3,350<br>11¼ | 4,400<br>17¼ | | | | |
| | | | | | | | | | |
| | | | 1,750 | | | | | | |
| | | | | | | | | | |
| | | 1,400<br>5 | | | | | | | |
| | | | | | | | | | |

## VIII.

*Table for Finding the Distance of an Object at Sea.* *

To use the table, let an observer from the cross-trees, measure the angle between the distant horizon and the enemy's water line, and look into the table with that angle; opposite to it, in the column marked distances, will be found the distance of the object in yards.

| Yards. | Height of the eye above the level of the sea, in feet. | | | | | | | | |
|---|---|---|---|---|---|---|---|---|---|
| Distance. | 20 | 30 | 40 | 50 | 60 | 70 | 80 | 90 | 100 |
|  | ° ′ | ° ′ | ° ′ | ° ′ | ° ′ | ° ′ | ° ′ | ° ′ | ° ′ |
| 100 | 8.44 | 5.37 | 7.29 | 9.21 | 11.11 | 13.00 | 14.47 | 16.34 | 18.16 |
| 200 | 1.50 | 2.46 | 3.43 | 4.39 | 5.35 | 6.31 | 7.27 | 8.23 | 9.18 |
| 300 | 1.12 | 1.49 | 2.26 | 3.04 | 3.41 | 4.19 | 4.56 | 5.33 | 6.11 |
| 400 | .52 | 1.21 | 1.48 | 2.16 | 2.44 | 3.12 | 3.40 | 4.08 | 4.36 |
| 500 | .41 | 1.03 | 1.25 | 1.48 | 2.10 | 2.32 | 2.54 | 3.17 | 3.39 |
| 600 | .34 | .52 | 1.10 | 1.29 | 1.47 | 2.05 | 2.24 | 2.42 | 3.01 |
| 700 | .28 | .44 | 1.01 | 1.15 | 1.31 | 1.46 | 2.01 | 2.18 | 2.34 |
| 800 | .24 | .38 | .51 | 1.05 | 1.18 | 1.32 | 1.46 | 2.00 | 2.13 |
| 900 | .21 | .33 | .45 | .57 | 1.09 | 1.22 | 1.33 | 1.45 | 1.57 |
| 1000 | .18 | .29 | .40 | .50 | 1.01 | 1.12 | 1.22 | 1.34 | 1.45 |
| 1100 | .16 | .26 | .35 | .45 | .55 | 1.05 | 1.15 | 1.24 | 1.34 |
| 1200 | .15 | .23 | .32 | .41 | .50 | .59 | 1.08 | 1.17 | 1.26 |
| 1300 | .13 | .21 | .29 | .37 | .45 | .53 | 1.02 | 1.10 | 1.18 |
| 1400 | .12 | .19 | .27 | .34 | .41 | .49 | .57 | 1.04 | 1.12 |
| 1500 | .11 | .18 | .24 | .31 | .38 | .45 | .52 | .59 | 1.07 |
| 1600 | .10 | .16 | .22 | .29 | .35 | .42 | .48 | .55 | 1.02 |
| 1700 | .09 | .15 | .21 | .27 | .33 | .39 | .45 | .51 | .58 |
| 1800 | .08 | .14 | .19 | .25 | .31 | .36 | .42 | .48 | .54 |
| 1900 | .08 | .13 | .18 | .23 | .29 | .34 | .39 | .45 | .50 |
| 2000 | .07 | .12 | .17 | .22 | .27 | .32 | .37 | .42 | .47 |
| 2100 | .06 | .11 | .16 | .20 | .25 | .30 | .35 | .40 | .45 |
| 2200 | .06 | .10 | .15 | .19 | .24 | .28 | .33 | .38 | .42 |
| 2300 | .05 | .10 | .14 | .18 | .22 | .27 | .31 | .36 | .40 |
| 2400 | .05 | .09 | .13 | .17 | .21 | .25 | .29 | .34 | .38 |
| 2500 | .05 | .08 | .12 | .16 | .20 | .24 | .28 | .32 | .36 |

No correct use of this table can be made when the proximity of land may interfere with the distance of the horizon.

---

* By Lieutenant W. P. Buckner, U. S. N.

## IX.

*Angles subtended by the mainmasts of British ships-of-war between the water-line and the truck, and also between the water-line and the topmast cross-trees, at distances expressed in yards, the eye of the observer being placed 20 feet above the level of the water.* (See Article 278, page 83.)

| DISTANCES. | SHIPS OF THE LINE. || || FRIGATES. || || SLOOPS. || BRIGS. ||
|---|---|---|---|---|---|---|---|---|---|---|---|---|
| | 120 Guns. 3 Decks. || From 92 to 80 Guns. 2 Decks. || 50 Guns. || 42 Guns. || 26 Guns. || 16 Guns. ||
| | Truck. 208 feet. | Cross-trees. 152 feet. | Truck. 198 feet. | Cross-trees. 144 feet. | Truck. 176 feet. | Cross-trees. 125 feet. | Truck. 168 feet. | Cross-trees. 120 feet. | Truck. 121 feet. | Cross-trees. 85 feet. | Truck. 125 feet. | Cross-trees. 65 feet. |
| Yds | ° ′ | ° ′ | ° ′ | ° ′ | ° ′ | ° ′ | ° ′ | ° ′ | ° ′ | ° ′ | ° ′ | ° ′ |
| 100 | 35 58 | 27 34 | 34 30 | 26 16 | 31 17 | 23 6 | 30 4 | 22 15 | 22 25 | 16 2 | 23 6 | 16 2 |
| 200 | 19 18 | 14 19 | 18 26 | 13 35 | 16 29 | 11 50 | 15 46 | 11 22 | 11 28 | 8 5 | 11 50 | 8 5 |
| 300 | 13 4 | 9 37 | 12 27 | 9 7 | 11 6 | 7 55 | 10 37 | 7 87 | 7 40 | 5 24 | 7 55 | 5 24 |
| 400 | 9 52 | 7 14 | 9 23 | 6 51 | 8 22 | 5 57 | 7 59 | 5 43 | 5 46 | 4 3 | 5 57 | 4 8 |
| 500 | 7 55 | 5 47 | 7 32 | 5 29 | 6 42 | 4 46 | 6 24 | 4 35 | 4 37 | 3 15 | 4 46 | 3 15 |
| 600 | 6 36 | 4 50 | 6 17 | 4 35 | 5 35 | 3 58 | 5 21 | 3 49 | 3 51 | 2 42 | 3 58 | 2 42 |
| 700 | 5 40 | 4 9 | 5 24 | 3 56 | 4 58 | 3 24 | 4 35 | 3 16 | 3 18 | 2 19 | 3 24 | 2 20 |
| 800 | 4 57 | 3 38 | 4 43 | 3 26 | 4 12 | 2 59 | 4 1 | 2 52 | 2 53 | 2 2 | 2 59 | 2 2 |
| 900 | 4 24 | 3 13 | 4 12 | 3 3 | 3 44 | 2 39 | 3 33 | 2 33 | 2 34 | 1 48 | 2 39 | 1 48 |
| 1000 | 3 58 | 2 54 | 3 57 | 2 45 | 3 22 | 2 28 | 3 12 | 2 17 | 2 19 | 1 37 | 2 23 | 1 37 |
| 1100 | 3 36 | 2 38 | 3 26 | 2 30 | 3 3 | 2 10 | 2 55 | 2 5 | 2 6 | 1 28 | 2 10 | 1 28 |
| 1200 | 3 18 | 2 25 | 3 9 | 2 17 | 2 48 | 1 59 | 2 40 | 1 55 | 1 56 | 1 21 | 1 59 | 1 21 |
| 1300 | 3 3 | 2 14 | 2 54 | 2 7 | 2 35 | 1 50 | 2 28 | 1 46 | 1 47 | 1 14 | 1 50 | 1 14 |
| 1400 | 2 50 | 2 4 | 2 42 | 1 58 | 2 24 | 1 42 | 2 18 | 1 38 | 1 39 | 1 9 | 1 42 | 1 10 |
| 1500 | 2 39 | 1 56 | 2 31 | 1 50 | 2 15 | 1 35 | 2 8 | 1 32 | 1 32 | 1 5 | 1 35 | 1 5 |

## X.—ANGLES SUBTENDED—

*Angles subtended by the mainmasts of French ships-of-war, water line and the topmast cross-trees, at distances ex- feet above the level of the water.*

| DISTANCES. | SHIPS OF THE LINE. | | | | | |
|---|---|---|---|---|---|---|
| | 120 Guns. | | 90 Guns. | | 82 Guns. | |
| | 220 feet. Truck. | 153 feet. Cross-trees. | 201 feet. Truck. | 151 feet. Cross-trees. | 192 feet. Truck. | 188 feet. Cross-trees. |
| Yards. | ° ′ | ° ′ | ° ′ | ° ′ | ° ′ | ° ′ |
| 100 | 37 30 | 28 31 | 34 55 | 27 24 | 33 38 | 24 50 |
| 200 | 20 20 | 14 51 | 18 41 | 14 13 | 17 54 | 13 2 |
| 300 | 13 43 | 9 59 | 12 38 | 9 33 | 12 5 | 8 44 |
| 400 | 10 25 | 7 31 | 9 32 | 7 11 | 9 6 | 6 34 |
| 500 | 8 21 | 6 1 | 7 39 | 5 45 | 7 13 | 5 16 |
| 600 | 6 59 | 5 1 | 6 23 | 4 48 | 6 5 | 4 23 |
| 700 | 5 59 | 4 18 | 5 28 | 4 7 | 5 14 | 3 46 |
| 800 | 5 14 | 3 46 | 4 48 | 3 36 | 4 35 | 3 18 |
| 900 | 4 39 | 3 21 | 4 16 | 3 12 | 4 4 | 2 56 |
| 1000 | 4 11 | 3 1 | 3 50 | 2 53 | 3 40 | 2 38 |
| 1100 | 3 49 | 2 44 | 3 29 | 2 37 | 3 20 | 2 26 |
| 1200 | 3 30 | 2 31 | 3 12 | 2 24 | 3 3 | 2 12 |
| 1300 | 3 14 | 2 19 | 2 57 | 2 13 | 2 49 | 2 2 |
| 1400 | 2 60 | 2 9 | 2 44 | 2 4 | 2 37 | 1 53 |
| 1500 | 2 48 | 2 1 | 2 33 | 1 55 | 2 27 | 1 45 |

## FRENCH VESSELS.

*between the water-line and the truck, and between the pressed in yards, the eye of the observer being placed 20*

| FRIGATES. | | | | CORVETTES. | | BRIGS. | |
|---|---|---|---|---|---|---|---|
| 60 Guns. | | 44 Guns. | | 24 Guns. | | 18 Guns. | |
| 188 feet. Truck. | 189 feet. Cross-trees. | 163 feet. Truck. | 121 feet. Cross-trees. | 120 feet. Truck. | 85 feet. Cross-trees. | 112 feet. Truck. | 77 feet. Cross-trees. |
| ° ′ | ° ′ | ° ′ | ° ′ | ° ′ | ° ′ | ° ′ | ° ′ |
| 33 4 | 25 27 | 30 4 | 22 25 | 22 15 | 16 2 | 20 52 | 14 34 |
| 17 33 | 13 7 | 15 46 | 11 28 | 11 22 | 8 5 | 10 37 | 7 20 |
| 11 51 | 8 48 | 10 37 | 7 40 | 7 37 | 5 24 | 7 6 | 4 54 |
| 8 55 | 6 87 | 7 59 | 5 46 | 5 43 | 4 8 | 5 20 | 8 40 |
| 7 9 | 5 18 | 6 24 | 4 87 | 4 35 | 3 15 | 4 16 | 2 56 |
| 5 58 | 4 25 | 5 21 | 3 51 | 3 49 | 2 42 | 3 34 | 2 27 |
| 5 6 | 3 47 | 4 35 | 3 18 | 3 16 | 2 19 | 3 3 | 2 6 |
| 4 29 | 3 19 | 4 1 | 2 53 | 2 52 | 2 2 | 2 40 | 1 50 |
| 3 59 | 2 57 | 3 83 | 2 34 | 2 33 | 1 48 | 2 23 | 1 38 |
| 3 35 | 2 39 | 3 12 | 2 19 | 2 17 | 1 37 | 2 8 | 1 28 |
| 3 16 | 2 25 | 2 55 | 2 6 | 2 5 | 1 28 | 1 57 | 1 20 |
| 2 59 | 2 13 | 2 40 | 1 56 | 1 55 | 1 21 | 1 47 | 1 14 |
| 2 46 | 2 2 | 2 28 | 1 47 | 1 46 | 1 14 | 1 39 | 1 8 |
| 2 34 | 1 54 | 2 18 | 1 39 | 1 38 | 1 10 | 1 32 | 1 3 |
| 2 24 | 1 46 | 2 8 | 1 32 | 1 32 | 1 5 | 1 26 | 0 59 |

# XI.—TANGENT

*Tangent practice with 8-inch and 32-pounder guns, with to the axis of the bore. The line supposed to be struck is*

| POINTS AIMED AT. | | 8-INCH GUN OF 68 CWT. *1 shell and 9lbs. powder.* | | | | 8-INCH GUN OF 55 CWT. *Charge 7 lbs. 1 shell.* | |
|---|---|---|---|---|---|---|---|
| In a French ship of 82 guns. | In a French frigate of 44 guns. | At the upper part of lower ports—gun deck. | About half way between rail and fore yard. | 8½ feet below mizen topmast cross-trees. | Above main truck. | Middle of lower deck ports. | 10 feet above hammock rail. |
| | | Middle of gun deck ports. | About midway between water and main cap. | Fore topmast cross-trees. | | Sills of gun-deck ports. | About midway between water and fore cap. |
| **Height of the parts aimed at above water.** Ft. In. | | 9  0 | 48  7 | 108  6 | 207  1 | 7  6 | 87  10 |
| **Distance.** Yards. | | 330 | 660 | 970 | 1260 | 283 | 579 |
| **Elevation.** Deg's. | | Level | 1 | 2 | 3 | Level | 1 |

NOTE.—This mode of firing presents serious disadvantages. The the enemy's vessel, the class of which can seldom be accurately to hit, and the chances of the ricochet are lost; hence tangent firing lating the elevation of the guns. The spars of English ships are rather

## PRACTICE.

*the charge for distant firing. The line of sight is parallel in the water-line.*

| Elevation | Range (yds) | Height | Point aimed at | Alternate |
|---|---|---|---|---|
| 2° | 639 | 79′ 8″ | Main top. | A little below main cap. |
| 3° | 1148 | 188′ 0″ | Just below main truck. | Above main truck. |

**32-POUNDER OF 57 CWT.  Charge 9 lbs. 1 shot.**

| Elevation | Range (yds) | Height | Point aimed at | Alternate |
|---|---|---|---|---|
| Level | 360 | 9′ 0″ | At upper part of lower deck ports. | Middle of gun-deck ports. |
| 1° | 760 | 48′ 9″ | About midway between main cap and water. | Just under fore yard. |
| 2° | 1150 | 129′ 6″ | 3 feet above fore topmast cross-trees. | Main topmast cap. |
| 3° | .... | .... | Above main truck. | |

**32-POUNDER OF 27 CWT.  Charge 4 lbs. 1 shot.**

| Elevation | Range (yds) | Height | Point aimed at | Alternate |
|---|---|---|---|---|
| Level | 250 | 7′ 0″ | Middle of lower deck ports. | Sills of gun-deck ports. |
| 1° | 545 | 35′ 6″ | About 10 feet above hammock rail. | Midway between water and main top. |
| 2° | 800 | 90′ 9″ | Main cap. | 6 feet above main cap. |
| 3° | 1047 | 171′ 6″ | Head of main top-gallant rigging. | Main truck. |

points aimed at have often to be estimated, as well as the distance of
determined; the men are taught to aim where they are not expected
should only be resorted to when there are no other means of regu-
less than those of French ships of the same class.

## RIFLED, 12-POUNDER BRONZE HOWITZER.

DISTANCE BETWEEN SIGHT BARS, 26.25 IN.

*8 feet, height.*

| Elevation. | Range. | Time. |
|---|---|---|
| | Yards. | Sec. |
| Point Blank.......... | 345 | 1.5 |
| 1°..................... | 705 | 2.3 |
| 2°..................... | 985 | 3.1 |
| 3°..................... | 1,150 | 4.0 |
| 4°..................... | 1,500 | 4.9 |
| 5°..................... | 1,750 | 5.8 |
| 6°..................... | 2,000 | 6.7 |
| 7°..................... | 2,240 | 7.6 |

## 12-POUNDER SMOOTH-BORE BRONZE HOWITZER.

DISTANCE BETWEEN SIGHT-BARS, 26.25 IN.

*8 feet, height.*

| Elevation. | Range. | Time. |
|---|---|---|
| | Yards. | Sec. |
| Point Blank.......... | 327 | 1.5 |
| 1°..................... | 563 | 2.1 |
| 2°..................... | 725 | 2.7 |
| 3°..................... | 856 | 3.3 |
| 4°..................... | 968 | 4.0 |
| 5°..................... | 1,070 | 4.8 |
| 6°..................... | 1,160 | 5.7 |

## SERVICE CHARGES FOR NAVAL GUNS.

| Guns. | | Charges. | | | Diameter of Cartridge Gauge. | Saluting. |
|---|---|---|---|---|---|---|
| Calibre. | Weight. | For distant firing, $\frac{1}{5}$th | For ordinary firing, $\frac{1}{6}$ths | For near firing, $\frac{2}{10}$ths. | | |
| 15-in. | 42,000 lbs. | 35 lbs. | 35 lbs. | 50 lbs. | .... | .... |
| | | | | | *Conical.* | |
| 11-in. | 15,700 " | 20 " | 15 " | 15 " | 11×5.5×11 | 7 lbs. |
| *10-in. | 16,000 " | 40 " | 35 " | 25 " | .... | .... |
| 10-in. | 12,000 " | 15 " | 12¼ " | 12¼ " | 10×5.0×10 | 6 " |
| 9-in. | 9,000 " | 13 " | 10 " | 10 " | 9×4.5×9 | 5 " |
| *8-in. | 10,000 " | 20 " | 16 " | 16 " | .... | .... |
| | | | | | *Cylindrical.* | |
| 8-in. | 68 cwt. | 9 " | 8 " | 6 " | 5.50 | 4.0 |
| *8-in. | 6,500 lbs. | 8 " | 7 " | 6 " | .... | .... |
| 8-in. | 55 cwt. | 7 " | 7 " | 6 " | 5.50 | 4.0 |
| 64-pdr. | 106 " | 16 " | 12 " | 8 " | 7.00 | 6.0 |
| 32-pdr. | 57 " | 9 " | 8 " | 6 " | 5.50 | 4.0 |
| 32-pdr. | 51 " | 8 " | 7 " | 5 " | 5.50 | 4.0 |
| 32-pdr. | 46 " | 7 " | 7 " | 5 " | 5.50 | 4.0 |
| *32-pdr. | 4,500 lbs. | 7 " | 7 " | 5 " | 5.50 | 4.0 |
| 32-pdr. | 42 cwt. | 6 " | 6 " | 4 " | 5.50 | 4.0 |
| 32-pdr. | 33 " | 4¼ " | 4¼ " | 4 " | 5.50 | 4.0 |
| 32-pdr. | 27 " | 4 " | 4 " | 3 " | 5.50 | 3.0 |

\* New models.

---

NOTE.—With the 15-inch guns at close quarters against iron-clads, 60 lbs. and a solid shot *may* be used for 20 rounds. So also with the 11-inch, 80 lbs. and a solid shot. With all the other guns, under like circumstances, and where penetration is desired, the *distant* firing charges should be substituted for the *near* firing.

## CHARGES FOR NAVY RIFLE GUNS.

| Gun. | ORDNANCE. | | | CHARGE. | | |
|---|---|---|---|---|---|---|
| | Calibre. | Diam. of bore. | Weight. | Weight. | Kind of powder. | Diameter of Cartridge Gauge. |
| | | inch. | lbs. | lbs. | | inch. |
| Parrott... | 150-pdr. | 8.00 | 16,500 | 16 | Rifle. | 7.00 |
| Do. ... | 100-pdr. | 6.40 | 9,700 | 10 | " | 5.50 |
| Do. ... | 60-pdr. | 5.30 | 4,900 | 6 | " | 4.60 |
| Do. ... | 30-pdr. | 4.20 | 3,550 | 8¼ | Cannon. | 3.70 |
| Do. ... | 20-pdr. | 3.67 | 1,750 | 2 | " | 3.25 |
| Dahlgren.. | 20-pdr. | 4.00 | 1,340 | 2 | " | .... |
| Do. .. | 12-pdr. | 3.40 | 880 | 1 | " | .... |

## WEIGHTS OF SHOT FOR NAVY GUNS.

### SMOOTH BORES.

| XV-in. || XI-in. | X-in. | IX-in. | VIII-in. | 32-pdr. |
| Cored. | Solid. | | | | | |
|---|---|---|---|---|---|---|
| 400 lbs. | 440 lbs. | 166 lbs. | 124 lbs. | 90 lbs. | 65 lbs. | 32.5 lbs. |

### RIFLES.

| Parrott. | 150-pdr. | 100-pdr. | 60-pdr. | 30-pdr. | 20-pdr. | |
|---|---|---|---|---|---|---|
| | 135 to 154 lbs. | 70 to 100 lbs. | 60 lbs. | 30 lbs. | 20 lbs. | .... |
| Dahlgren. | .... | 20-pdr. | 12-pdr. | .... | .... | .... |
| | .... | 20 lbs. | 12 lbs. | .... | .... | .... |

## WEIGHTS OF SHELLS FOR NAVY GUNS.
### SMOOTH BORES.

| Calibre. | XV-in. | XI-in. | X-in. | IX-in. | VIII-in. | 32-pdr. |
|---|---|---|---|---|---|---|
| Empty.... | lbs. 330 | lbs. 127 | lbs. 95 | lbs. 68.50 | lbs. 50. | lbs. 25.0 |
| Filled and Sabotted. | 352 | 135.5 | 101.50 | 73.50 | 52.75 | 26.50 |

## BURSTING CHARGES FOR NAVY SHELLS.

### RIFLES.

| Parrott.... | 150-pdr. | 100-pdr. | 60-pdr. | 30-pdr. | 20-pdr. | |
|---|---|---|---|---|---|---|
| | 135 lbs. | 80 to 100 lbs. | 50 lbs. | 29 lbs. | 18 lbs. | .... |
| Dahlgren.. | 20-pdr. | 12-pdr. | .... | .... | .... | .... |
| | 18 lbs. | 11 lbs. | .... | .... | .... | .... |

## BURSTING CHARGES FOR NAVY SHELLS.

### SMOOTH BORES.

| XV-in. | XI-in. | X-in. | IX-in. | 8-in. | 32-pdr. | Howitzer. | |
| | | | | | | 24-pdr. | 12-pdr. |
|---|---|---|---|---|---|---|---|
| lbs. 18. | lbs. 6.00 | lbs. 4.00 | lbs. 3.00 | lbs. 1.85 | lbs. 0.90 | lbs. 1.00 | lbs. 0.50 |

### RIFLES.

| | PARROTT. | | | | DAHLGREN. | |
| 150-pdr. | 100-pdr. | 60-pdr. | 30-pdr. | 20-pdr. | 20-pdr. | 12-pdr. |
|---|---|---|---|---|---|---|
| lbs. Long....10.81 Short... 4.81 | lbs. 5.81 3.69 | lbs. 3.25 2.12 | lbs. 1.5 .... | lbs. 1.0 .... | lbs. 0.86 .... | lbs. 0.50 .... |

## CONTENTS AND WEIGHTS OF SPHERICAL SHRAPNEL FOR NAVY GUNS.

| Calibre. | Weight of Empty Shell. | Contents. | | | Weight Complete. |
|---|---|---|---|---|---|
| | | No. of Balls. | lbs. of Sulphur. | Bursting Charge. | |
| | lbs. | *Lead.* | lbs. | oz. | lbs. |
| 12-pdr | 6.50 | 80 | 0.75 | 0.80 | 12.00 |
| 24-pdr | 11.00 | 175 | 1.50 | 1.08 | 24.00 |
| 32-pdr | 15.00 | 235 | 2.00 | 1.25 | 32.00 |
| | | *Iron.* | | | |
| VIII-inch | 29.00 | 210 | 5.00 | 2.50 | 52.00 |
| IX-inch | 38.00 | 325 | 7.00 | 3.00 | 75.00 |
| X-inch | 57.00 | 435 | 8.50 | 4.00 | 101.00 |
| XI-inch | 76 00 | 625 | 10.00 | 6.00 | 141.00 |
| XV-inch | 178.00 | 1,000 | 30.00 | 10.00 | 356.00 |

## CONTENTS AND WEIGHTS OF CANISTER FOR NAVY SMOOTH-BORE GUNS.

| Calibre. | Contents. | | Weight. | |
|---|---|---|---|---|
| | Size of Balls. | No. of Balls. | Lead. | Iron. |
| | | | lbs. | lbs. |
| 12-pdr | 1-in..Lead or Iron. | 89 | 11.0 | 9.00 |
| 24-pdr | 1.30.. " " | 89 | 22.0 | 17.00 |
| 32-pdr | 1.30..Iron. | 100 | .... | 30.00 |
| VIII-inch | 1.30.. " | 162 | .... | 50.00 |
| IX-inch | 1.30.. " | 220 | .... | 69.00 |
| X-inch | 1.30.. " | 268 | .... | 101.00 |
| XI-inch | 1.30.. " | 390 | .... | 120.00 |
| XV-inch | 1.30.. " | 800 | .... | 250.00 |

www.ingramcontent.com/pod-product-compliance
Lightning Source LLC
Chambersburg PA
CBHW031824230426
43669CB00009B/1222